The Shaman's Gift

The Shaman's Gift

Lee Fishman

TransMedia Press
Philadelphia, PA

Library of Congress Cataloging – Publication Data on File

978-1-7364787-1-4
ebook ISBN 978-1-7364787-0-7

www.leefishman.net

TransMedia Press
Philadelphia, PA

To the people of Belize and to many friends there,
thanks for sharing your hospitality,
your wisdom and your knowledge.

One

A cure for cancer? Did he really just say that? Mel Powers'
strident tones resonated across the courtyard where he sat
beside a large palm, one he'd had his employees dig up, stick
in a pot and lug on to the veranda. "Just setting the stage," he'd
said with a wink, placing the foliage next to his throne-like
rattan chair. "Gotta give 'em a little show biz."

A high fence encircled the compound, separating the main
house, staff quarters and the newly built lab from the steamy
Belize rainforest surrounding it. Howler monkeys screeched in
the trees overhead. Tropical vines swayed in a breeze that did
little to cool the air. At the far end of the property, a muddy river
flowed past, carrying the occasional crocodile.

Mel, in bush jacket, shorts and boots, faced the camera, happy
to expound on his latest venture. "Throughout my career, I've
used technology to make the world a better place. Now I plan
to do the same thing in the laboratory."

Standing at an open window inside that still unfinished lab, I took in every word, and my mind reeled. Around me, equipment sat untouched. Boxes, still unpacked, had arrived just days before, trucked in from Belize City airport on the only road leading from the coast to the jungle interior. Oh God, Carrie. *What did you get yourself into?*

"Please, please. Don't let them come in here," I whispered.

An assistant adjusted the mic attached to Mel's collar and the filmmaker continued her questioning. "Before pulling up stakes in the U. S. and relocating to Belize, you were best known as a high-flying tech entrepreneur. Is it possible that this new emphasis on science may be beyond your reach?"

"Some people might say that," Mel responded. "But I disagree. To help in this endeavor, I've hired a knowledgeable young scientist, Dr. Carrie Mullen. Together, we're looking at some cutting-edge research. This could be the beginning of the most important work of my life."

What is that work? I still don't know.

When we first met, Mel mentioned the economic development grant he'd received from the Belize government and I was flattered that he wanted to know about my own projects. His intense blue eyes, below a wild shock of dark hair, lasered in on me as I told him of the months I'd spent studying the medicinal properties of jungle plants. He was full of questions, eager to know the ways of native healers who used them. Half an hour later he said, "Carrie, I want you to come work for me. Be part of my team."

If I wanted to stay in Belize and continue my own research, I needed to do something and fast. *Why not say yes?*

After that we never really agreed on what the initial project might be. And, for sure, he'd never said a word about cancer. Now here was the filmmaker sent by the Belize Economic Development Agency, making what she called a 'video progress report and what Mel privately called harassment.

Back on the porch, the filmmaker continued her questions. "Can you provide any details on the scope of this new venture?"

"The need for confidentiality prevents me from commenting further," he replied. From where I lurked near the window, I could hear the annoyance in Mel's response. "I'm sure you understand that a timetable on any scientific discovery would be impossible to provide at this point."

Did Mel know he'd gone too far? Peeking out the window, I saw him pull off the mic. Then he stood, waving his hand back and forth, motioning to cut.

Beads of sweat bloomed on my forehead. *How did I get here?*

I blink, and I am again nineteen. A college junior, I'd barely heard of the small Central American country of Belize. But when Jeff Donnelly, my favorite professor at the University of Illinois announced his summer session "for credit field trip", I was all-in. Majoring in bio, I planned to apply for med school. So, what could be better than a six-week trek into the rainforest? It sounded like a cool way to earn a few extra credits, and it might look good on the med school application.

Backpacks slung over shoulders; we were a small group of nerdy undergrads excited to be heading off on a scientific adventure. Spirits were high as we made our way through customs at the small Belize City airport. Outside we piled onto a brightly decorated school bus that would whisk us out of a gritty urban environment into a green, green, very green world. Civilization fell away as we bumped along the open road, past a forest dotted with small wooden houses painted tropical hues of coral, lavender, and yellow. Nearby, corn grew in the fields next to livestock penned in rough-hewn corrals. Crepe myrtle bushes punctuated the dusty road with their magenta blooms.

Off the bus, in the remote town of San Ignacio, Jeff pointed to a sign in front of a small two-story house. It read *Jungle Remedies* in bold print with treatments promised for cancer, prostate, diabetes, and more. With the proprietor's name unadorned by the title of Doctor or MD, I'd half expected Dr. Jeff to turn up his nose. Instead, he respectfully explained the traditions of the indigenous people and their belief in folk healers.

Once we found our bunks at the student hostel, we were ready to explore the town, celebrating our arrival with a boisterous dinner at an outdoor café. When Jeff warned of the dawn wake-up call, there were groans all around but, next morning, I congratulated myself for not drinking more than one beer with dinner.

Excited for our first foray into the wild, we were awed by the canopy of dense vegetation overhead. The earth, springy below our feet, was vibrant with the rich odors of growing things. From above, monkeys expressed displeasure at our presence with screeches of protest. As Jeff led the way, I tried to stay close, scribbling notes as he spoke and picking samples of the plants he pointed out. In less than an hour, the intense heat and humidity left us drenched with sweat.

After the first week, we met with a local healer who led us along forest trails, identifying the medicinal plants in a mixture of Spanish and English. Later, he took us to his small workshop where we gathered around for a hands-on lesson showing us how to dry the plants we'd harvested. The next day we ground some of the leaves into a powder. Others we boiled into tea over the open fire.

Midway into our trip, Jeff drove us to the home of a native midwife. But before he could make the introductions, a battered truck drove up. With a few words in Spanish, the driver helped his very pregnant wife down from the front seat and up the steps into the midwife's small house. Anticipating the entrance of a new life into the world, Jeff shooed us over to a shady spot away from the house. There we stood nervous and excited, hoping to see the midwife in action.

All eyes were on the young father-to-be as he smoked and paced the rickety porch. The only sounds were birds squawking as they flitted from tree to tree. Then a harsh scream pierced the hush as the young mother howled in pain. Finally, after many tense moments, a baby's first cry broke the spell. Then silence.

As we eyeballed each other, afraid to speak, the midwife appeared at the door, motioning for Jeff to come to her. In rapid Spanish, she pointed him to a banana tree at the edge of the clearing. Then she handed him a machete and a shallow pan. Our mouths dropped open, but Jeff didn't flinch. Quick off the mark, he hacked pieces from the roots of the tree, and within minutes he hopped back on the porch, with chopped pieces of the banana tree root.

Jeff pulverized the fibrous material, with a mortar and pestle, his face crimson with exertion. *"Hola! Señora, aqui."*

The midwife came back out with a pot of steaming water, pouring it over the plant fibers to clean them. That done, he strained the liquid into a cup and knocked again on the doorframe. The midwife stuck out her hand and took the liquid.

When she reappeared minutes later, the young father's eyes were rooted on her face. The two spoke rapidly in a tongue that wasn't Spanish. Was it Mayan, perhaps? She beckoned him inside. After a tense few minutes, the new father emerged grinning widely, and we all cheered and high-fived.

Later, Jeff said, "I know that was tense, but you guys did well."

We peppered him with questions. "What did she do?" "What happened?"

"The baby was born fine and healthy. But after the delivery, the mother was hemorrhaging," Jeff said. "She was losing a lot of blood. The sap of the banana tree roots stopped the bleeding that could have claimed her life."

As the trip progressed, I saw an herbal poultice draw infection from the red and swollen foot of an injured child. When a fellow student fell ill with bronchitis, immediate relief came from a salve made from leaves and berries found in the forest. Another student who sprained an ankle out in the bush found that a bandage made from the leaves of a plant called pheasant tail brought him relief. On our next to the last night, I burned my hand flipping burgers at an outdoor barbecue. With the application of leaves from the wild coco, the blisters quickly subsided.

I found myself fascinated with the folk healers and their abilities. On the flight back to the States, I snagged the seat next to Jeff. He dozed for most of the trip, but before we touched down in Chicago, I told him that I'd found my true calling in the rainforest. "I appreciate your enthusiasm, Carrie," he said. His brown eyes, peering over wire-rimmed specs, looked deep into mine. I felt thrilled and flattered by his sincerity. "But sometimes, when you take a trip like this, you become fascinated by a country. It's like when you go on a vacation to a beautiful place and then decide you'd like to live there. It's almost a fantasy, but if you actually did it, you might find the reality quite different."

I nodded wordlessly, but I knew what I was feeling was real. From then on, I was hooked. And those were the words I used when I told my parents that, after graduation, I didn't want to go to medical school after all.

It took me years of hard work to get a Ph.D. in ethnobotany. The more I learned, the more I wanted to become part of a growing academic community that felt indigenous healers and their natural plant remedies should be valued by science.

Online I found a citation for an article written years earlier. The blurb gave a brief description of the skills of a well-known Maya healer named Don Rodrigo Montoya. Curious to know more, I chased down the bound copy of the old botanical journal in the library stacks. Feeling proud of myself for finding it, I dug out the dusty volume then plunked down on a library stool to read every word. The author, a botanist, praised the indigenous healer's knowledge and generosity in treating the local people who sought his help.

Sadly, the writer ended with an alarming conclusion. He feared that the knowledge of the well-known shaman, known to everyone as Don Rodrigo, would be lost unless it was passed along to an apprentice. As I read those words, a wild idea popped into my head. *Could I become that apprentice?*

The article and what I'd read about the shaman stayed with me. More than anything, I wanted to meet him and learn about his traditional healing practices. I became determined to return to Belize. My friends called me crazy, but it became my goal.

When I shared this thought with Jeff, now my Ph.D. advisor, he laughed. "Carrie, I remember you said that once before, but I thought you would have moved on by now. Maybe you could try to get a grant, maybe even go to Belize for a research project. But live there? I don't know. Not to change the subject but, I just heard about a great job. They're hiring for a research staff position at the Brooklyn Botanical Garden. I have a good friend there, and I'd be happy to write you a reference if you're interested."

I shook my head. "Thanks for the job tip, but this is what I want to do, and it seems like Belize would be the place to go."

"You know Belize has changed," Jeff said. "I've heard that the poverty is still the same. They're still struggling to make economic progress, but in the last few years, they've lost a lot of the rainforest to slash and burn farming. That and the increased drug trafficking from Guatemala has also taken a toll."

Like Jeff, my parents were also against the trip. "Belize? Why would you want to go live there?" my mother asked. "You always said you wanted to be a doctor."

"I still do, Mom. Just a different kind of doctor."

"But it's dangerous, and there's so much poverty down there. And you'll be trudging around the jungle, hip-deep in mud."

My father took a different approach. "You are entitled to make your own decisions," he said. Still, he continually presented me with State Department warnings and travel advisories describing dangers lurking in Central America. "You know we'll always support you, no matter what you decide. But I hope you'll come to your senses."

The small inheritance my grandmother left me had been sitting in the bank since she died a few years before. Without that money, the trip would have been impossible. In my heart, I believed she would have been glad she was helping to make my dream a reality.

"You're over twenty-one," Dad said. "The money's yours to use as you see fit."

Growing up, my father would often tell me, "Carrie, you look just like your grandmother. And you're stubborn like her, too." I always felt strangely pleased when he said that. Even now I could still picture her smiling face and the twinkle in her eye. As a kid, I loved spending time with her. She'd dig out her old photo albums and we'd spend time looking at them together. Pointing to pictures of herself as a young college student, she'd remind me that my green eyes and thick auburn hair were just like hers. My favorite snapshots were of her with her students from the years she'd spent teaching high school science in the Chicago public schools.

I remember her saying, "There weren't many women in the science department when I started out. Sometimes, in the faculty lunchroom, the male teachers would ignore me. But once I made my mind up, I wouldn't let anything stop me. By the time I retired, I was head of the science curriculum committee for the entire school system." Looking back on those moments I hoped she'd approve of the way I'd chosen to use her money.

Two

Fresh off the airplane, in Belize City, I did my best to shrug off what I was leaving behind, a world still recovering from the financial crisis of 2008 and ongoing strife in the Middle East. Hopeful young people had elected Barack Obama to the White House. But unemployment was rampant and gas prices were running close to four dollars a gallon.

I made my way to San Ignacio, a small town near the Guatemalan border. On a map, it looked close to the village of San Mateo, the village where Don Rodrigo made his home, and I was determined to get there. After settling in at a local hotel, I found a taxi stand with a driver who knew where I wanted to go. *"Sí, Señorita* Everyone knows Don Rodrigo. I can take you to him for ten dollars American."* Grateful that the driver seemed to know the way to the farm, I agreed. Only later did I laugh at myself, as I came to realize how much I overpaid.

Driving the backroads, the village of San Mateo would have

been easy to miss. There was only a small grocery with one gas pump, a few small houses and a roadside stand where two women sold vegetables and handmade crafts. The driver turned off at the end of the dirt road and for the hundredth time, I questioned myself, wondering if what I hoped to do made any sense. My heart fluttered as a traditional Mayan house with a roof of thatched palm came into view. It was nestled between vegetable gardens on one side and a small barn on the other.

An old man sat on the small front porch, dressed in a faded shirt and well-patched pants. As he stood and waved to the driver, he couldn't have appeared more modest.

I waved. *"Buenos dias. Señor Montoya?"*

He eyed me quizzically as I emerged from the taxi. *"Buenos dias, Señorita?* How can I help you? Are you ill?"

"No, I wanted to meet you," I said.

"Visitors are always welcome, and I am not busy today."

The driver called out, *"Señorita,* do you want me to wait for you?" When I nodded, he turned off the engine, pulling his hat down over his eyes for a siesta.

Don Rodrigo beckoned, telling me he liked speaking with Americans. "Come in. I will make us some tea." Near the door was a wood-fired adobe stove. Metal pans hung from pegs on the wall. He led me to a small wooden table and offered a chair. And I spent a pleasant hour, sipping hibiscus tea and learning about how he came to Belize as a young man.

When he asked where I was staying, I told him of the small hotel in San Ignacio. He clucked his tongue. "By yourself?" he asked. *"Señorita,* be careful. Sometimes, I hear about people selling the drugs there."

After that first social call, I visited two or three times a week, making a pest of myself, turning up uninvited. Those early months, I couldn't even be sure he knew my name. More than once, he'd ask, "But why are you here, *Señorita?"*

"What do you want of me?" I would tell him then of my desire to study with him. But my words seemed to fall on deaf ears. Other times he would wave me away like a pesky fly. "I have no time for you today. I must go to the forest and go quickly. You will slow me down."

It took weeks before the elderly herbalist would tolerate my presence, but I wasn't willing to give up. Often, I tried to tell him that my work would not only help him, but it would have value for others. "There are many who believe in your natural healing ways and want to learn more about them," I said.

Finally, after a hot day spent together watering his crops, he turned with a sigh, asking, "What is it you wish to know?"

I almost cried. "If you will let me learn from you, I will work hard and record all I can."

"Why?"

"To make sure your work will not be lost."

Once Don Rodrigo agreed that I could study with him, he made a place for me to stay in a little shed next to the barn. "You will be safe here," he said. That first steamy night, I tried hard to get comfortable in the woven red and blue hammock. As I drifted off, something flew close to my head. Flicking on my flashlight, I screamed, horrified at the sight of a bat circling the rafters. Hearing my cries, Don Rodrigo soon appeared armed with a broom. Once he'd chased the bat from the shed; he reminded me to close the door against other intruders.

My next adventure came a few days later. I found a large metal tub in the barn and thought a bath would help rinse away the muddy residue I'd accumulated from digging in the garden. Don Rodrigo laughed then, pointing to the large plastic bucket I could use to draw up the water from the well. Sleeping in a hammock and bathing in a metal tub were details I chose to keep to myself when I had the chance to connect with my parents. I could only imagine how they would react, asking me,

"Is this why we put you through grad school?"

Those days were rough, but the rewards were real. Each day, I trailed Don Rodrigo, working by his side, days blending into weeks, time passing as if in a dream. We were a funny-looking pair. Even with his hat on, I stood almost a head taller than his five-foot frame. But his appearance was deceiving. As the rising sun heated everything it touched, it was hard to keep up as I followed him on his early morning treks to gather herbs

Later in the day there might be villagers seeking treatment. As the old healer gently examined those who came to him for help, I watched and listened as he first explained each diagnosis, later describing how he would treat the condition. Then it was time to prepare the plant-based treatments. On quiet days, when no patients sought him out, I tried to make myself useful, tending the crops, watering the garden, and caring for the goats and chickens.

A few times, scientists from other countries visited the farm to speak with Don Rodrigo. During those meetings, I always felt proud to be part of the process, joining the conversation as they all spoke on the porch or following behind the researchers as he took them on his rounds, gathering plants in the forest.

Sadly, as time passed, I began to see a change in my teacher. The light in his eyes was growing a little dimmer. Up in years, there was a slowness in his step. Often dispirited, he would ask, "Who will continue my work, when I can no longer do it?"

He told me he'd often tried to convince younger family members to carry on his traditions but with no luck. As time passed, I became fearful that my elderly teacher would perish before I'd recorded the full extent of his knowledge. More than once, I heard him say, "*Los jovenes,* the young people, only want to leave the villages. They go to the towns where they have *la música, la televisión, los teléfonos.*"

"You shouldn't blame them," I said. "They're just teenagers. All young people are attracted to the modern gadgets. They want all of those things. To get them, they must earn money. They need jobs, and it's hard to find them here in the country."

One steamy day in late summer, a battered white sedan pulled into Don Rodrigo's farmyard. I waved "hello" and called to him through the open door, "Maestro, you have a patient."

A short, stocky woman with a determined look emerged from the passenger's seat. Following behind her, a handsome, square-jawed young man with dark, shiny hair pulled suitcases and a battered guitar-case from the car's trunk. "Who are you?" she asked. "Where's the old man?" Not waiting for an answer, she brushed past me into the house. "*Papacito. Papacito.* We are here."

At first, Don Rodrigo seemed pleased by the new arrivals. However, he soon began to exhibit signs of annoyance, especially with his granddaughter, Josefina, hovering over him. From that day, life on Don Rodrigo's farm lost its peaceful rhythm.

One night, I heard him raise his voice, something he rarely did, "Josefina, *mi hija,* there is no money. Do you not under-stand? The wealth is in the plants."

"But *Abuelo*, how can this be? You are famous. Everyone knows you. The gringos, they write about you in books. Did they not give you money?"

At his soft-spoken "No," she stormed out into the tropical darkness, slamming the door behind her.

Josefina, undeterred, continued to insist that there were profits hidden from her somewhere on the farm. Suspicious that I was there to steal from the family, she began following me around as I did my chores.

During my teacher's afternoon siesta, I often went to the barn to check on the drying herbs. One day, Josefina must have followed me inside. Hearing her voice from behind. I jumped.

"Oh, you scared me."

" *Señorita?* I wish to speak to you."

"I didn't hear you. I thought I was alone."

"Is this where you hide the money?" she asked.

"What money?"

"The money my grandfather has made from the gringos coming to talk to him. I know they record his secrets and sell them to outsiders."

"*Señora*, you've seen how your grandfather lives. The people come with love in their hearts but little money. They might give him a chicken, some fruit, a bag of rice. He only asks for what they can give. You see how we eat the vegetables that we grow here."

"You are very clever. You sell the words of my grandfather and make money in secret that you hide from him. But you do not it hide from me." She turned and stalked off, puffs of dust following her heel prints.

I couldn't help noticing that Julio, the young man who arrived with Josefina, received a very different welcome. The old man's eyes lit up whenever he appeared. "Julio, *mi hijo*, come play something for us on your guitar."

Of all the family, only Julio, Don Rodrigo's young great-nephew, seemed to understand and believe in the wisdom of the plants. This was the knowledge I'd labored to record in notebooks and, even more, inside my head.

One evening after a simple meal of beans and tortillas flavored with sweet peppers from the garden, I sat on the porch with Julio and his uncle enjoying a cool breeze. Josefina had gone to the village.

"Julio, I dreamed of you last night. You have been chosen and I want to pass the knowledge to you. The plants must speak to you," Don Rodrigo said.

"Uncle, I understand, and I thank you for the honor. You say I can do this, but I'm afraid. I don't know if I have the strength to do this work."

"Do not let the world outside distract you with the cell phones and the music that plays in your ears." He pointed to the headphones slung around Julio's neck.

Julio hung his head. "I love the forest and the traditions of our people. I regret the time that I should have spent here with you, learning more."

Don Rodrigo nodded. "When I was young like you, I felt the same way. But one night I had a dream. And in that dream, my father passed his knowledge to me. Sadly, I have no son. My wife is dead, my daughter also. You are like the son that I don't have."

Julio looked down, "Uncle, I'm so sorry."

"It's not too late. If you try, our ancestors will help you. But you must be strong. "

"How can I even start?" Julio asked.

"First, you must fast three days and three nights and sleep outside under the stars. Pay close attention to your dreams. They will guide you. After that, stay close so that we can talk. Can you do that?"

"I will try."

"If you do, you will feel yourself wake up with the wisdom in your heart and in your hands. And that is the wisdom of the people, our people. Don't let it die."

"I will try, my Uncle," Julio said. He bent his head in respect. Don Rodrigo leaned close.

When he placed both hands on the young man's head in a blessing, my heart ached. If only he would bless me in the same way.

"If you do, I will give you the farm," the old man whispered.

"Only promise me you will not tell Josefina."

If Don Rodrigo had been his strong, robust self, it wouldn't have surprised me if he threw his granddaughter out. But Rodrigo was losing ground. I'd seen it coming for weeks. Early on, our morning walks in the forest had left me staggering after him as three or four times a week, we went out to collect plants, stalks, leaves, flowers, the herbal treasures that he used for healing. But on our last walk together, a coughing fit left him breathless. Even after resting while he chewed coca leaves to revive himself, we still were forced to turn back.

Secretly, I hoped that someday I might be able to buy some land and set up a healing space of my own. My Spanish was getting more than good, and I'd even picked up a few words of the Mayan tongue, Q'eché. Still, I knew it was crazy for me to believe I could make a place among the native people who sought out Don Rodrigo's help. I tried to hold on to that hope, but with his family circling in wait of an inheritance, any conflict would only bring harm.

Don Rodrigo seemed convinced that in time, his nephew would take on the mantle, take his place among his people. I felt better knowing that Julio might agree to stay. Still, I could see reluctance on Julio's part.

As I was dipping water from the well one morning, I heard a groan. There was Julio rubbing his head. "What's wrong? You look stressed."

"I have a headache. Too much tension, *la familia*. You know."

"Take a walk with me. I want to show you where we pick the rue. It's good for a headache."

Not far down the forest path, I pointed to the rue and snipped off a few of the small leafy branches. "If you soak these leaves in alcohol and rub the liquid on your head, it will help.

17

It's good for headaches and backaches."

"It might take more than that to help me get rid of the pain in my head," he laughed.

"I get it. You are feeling pressured. But, Julio, you are the best hope for your uncle. Don Rodrigo has been generous with his help to me. But you are the one who can truly carry on his work. Do you agree?"

"Thank you, *Señorita*. I'm honored, but I don't know if this is the life I want. I'm not sure. Some of my friends call him the sorcerer. They say that my uncle practices black magic."

Don Rodrigo, a sorcerer? No way! That's crazy. But I could understand his fears. "Black magic? No. Not Don Rodrigo. His heart is filled with kindness. Many times, I've heard people ask him to cast spells or use his knowledge for something that might bring harm. He always refuses to do it. Maybe you need some time to think about it."

"And I need a real job," Julio said. "I can't stay here anymore. There's no room and I'm tired of sleeping in the car. I found a little place for rent above the café where I play on the weekend. The owner says he will rent it to me pretty cheap, but I need money. I'm broke."

Walking back from the forest, I saw the raised plots of the farm's vegetable garden, the hens scratching in the yard and the little house. *I've loved calling this place home for the many months I've been here. But now my time at the farm is coming to an end, and it hurts.*

I tossed and turned in what seemed to be an endless night. The conflict with Josefina and fears for my teacher's fragility kept me awake. *Even with what I've accomplished, I'm not family. Maybe it's better if I leave.*

I needed to call home but, in the remote area where we lived, the cell phone signal was often weak. When I asked Julio to drive me to an internet café in San Ignacio, he agreed, offering kindly to wait outside while I made my call.

"Dad, Don Rodrigo's family came to stay. And now I feel like there's no place for me here anymore."

"Then why not come home," he said. "Do the work back in the States."

"Dad, you don't understand."

Part of me believed that if I left, it would all vanish. Even though I still had some of Gram's money left, I was surprised when my father offered to send me a few thousand dollars to live on for a few months more while I made up my mind.

"Send it to the Seven Sisters Lodge. I know the lodge owners, James and Gloria. They're good people and I trust them. I can stay there for a while. Give myself time to think."

'I'll do it just this once," he said. "But after that, if things don't work out, I want you to promise me that you'll come home."

"Dad, I better go. Your call is breaking up," I said. On the other end, my father waited in the silence for the promise I couldn't give, and the line went dead.

As the sun burned away the dawn mist, I spent one last morning going into the forest to gather plants with my teacher. Later, I pushed my clothes into a backpack and my notebooks into boxes. Going outside, I joined Don Rodrigo as he sat quietly on the porch. Together we watched as bees buzzed around the purple clumps of periwinkle. The jungle was still, the birds silent. Finally, the time came to say goodbye.

Unable to believe it was happening, I was hard-pressed to find the words. Instead, I bent low, kissing the back of his head in respect. As tears began to fall, I choked out a farewell, "I'll be close if you need me."

The old man gently wiped a tear from my cheek. "I will miss you, my child." His eyes looked tired.

With a backward glance and a murmured 'goodbye', I climbed into Julio's battered white sedan, and he drove me to the Seven Sisters Lodge.

Three

I missed the life I led at Don Rodrigo's farm but once I checked in at the Seven Sisters, I had to admit there were advantages. At the lodge, the flowers were fragrant, the sheets clean, and the morning buffet bountiful.

Living in the bush meant always being at the mercy of the elements. Even after my father sent me a satellite phone, the service would go out unexpectedly. Now I was able to make calls and even use my laptop with ease.

It was over a year since my last short trip home. And it felt good to be able to hear my father's voice clearly as I brought him up to date on what was happening.

"Who is he?"

"His name is Mel Powers. We met the first day I checked in at the lodge. I was talking to James, the lodge owner. Then Mel came over, all excited. He had this roll of architectural drawings under his arm. When he spread them out on a table in the lobby, I couldn't resist peeking over his shoulder. He asked James to go with him out to see the site."

"You shouldn't talk to strangers."

"Dad, please, I'm not ten years old. Let me finish. The first thing about the drawings that got my attention was a building marked lab. I was so curious about it that I asked a few questions. That's when he offered to let me tag along with James. We all piled into his Jeep and headed out to see the new compound taking shape in the jungle.

"The house was complete, the interior still unfurnished but the work was impressive. When he pointed out the lab, I was more than surprised. It measured 800 square feet."

"Be careful, kiddo," Dad said before he rang off.

The following evening in the lodge dining room, guests were lining up at the buffet. As I grabbed a plate, I saw Mel close behind in the line. We started talking and as I made my way to a free table out on the veranda, he followed. "May I?" He gestured to an empty chair. I nodded. "Please." The conversation continued over dinner.

"Tell me a little bit about yourself," he said.

"I've been here in Belize on and off for almost three years. I came here drawn to the country, the pristine forest and what I'd heard about a native healer, Don Rodrigo. I have a Ph.D. in ethnobotany."

"Ethnobotany? What's that?"

"Study of the use of plants by native peoples. My dissertation was on the use of medicinal plants among the Iroquois tribes. Years ago, I planned to go to med school, but I changed my mind. I want to combine my beliefs in the body's ability to heal itself with support from the natural world."

"Help from the natural world?"

"Yes, with plants providing aid in that healing."

"Hmmm," he said, taking a sip of water. "Interesting."

He's really listening. I felt energized for the first time in many days.

"What do you know about medical practice laws in Belize?" Mel asked.

"Like a lot of other things, pretty laissez-faire. It's not like back in the States. There are no laws regarding who may practice in this country. With medical doctors so scarce, people in the countryside turn to their traditional healers who practice freely."

He smiled, seeming to like that answer. "Where do you see yourself in five years?"

I looked at him in disbelief. *What? Is this some kind of job interview? Are you really gonna ask me that old chestnut of a question?*

I hid my surprise, "I hope to be right here in Belize, helping people. Continuing to learn more about the healing nature of plants."

"Do you consider yourself a hands-on kind of person?"

"Yes, Don Rodrigo taught me the power of healing touch."

Mel turned toward the forest where the songs of the birds, cicadas and frogs filled the night. "Here's where I want the magic to happen," he said.

Magic?

Mel stood. "Let's go to the lobby where there's more light," he said. "I want to show you something." I followed and we found chairs on either side of a lamp. From his backpack he produced more drawings. Spreading them out, he pointed to the lab.

"This is what I call 'the healing place'. I want you to bring all your skills and knowledge of the plants to the work. Maybe even bring in your healer if he is willing."

My head was spinning. *Don Rodrigo?*

"My goal is to help the people of Belize, the indigenous people. I feel I have a spiritual connection to them and to this land also. It feels like a karmic debt, you might say. Does that make sense? Someday, I'll tell you why."

"Tell me how I would fit into this?"

"Did I mention that I got a grant from the Belize Office of Economic Development?"

"Oh, congratulations. James mentioned that you've been an entrepreneur for many years. What are your plans for this venture?" I asked trying to steer back toward solid ground, hoping to move the conversation back to the lab.

Rustling through his files, Mel found a list he got from a biologist back in the States. Red checkmarks highlighted basic equipment already ordered. "It's still taking shape, but the elements, so far, are pretty much in sync with the type of research you've been delving into since you've been here."

"Do you mean the traditional medicine of the healers?"

"Yes, that's it exactly. And for that I need your expertise as a scientist. And I'd love to talk to your teacher."

"It sounds like an exciting plan."

Dad help me out here. I tried channeling my father.

What should I ask?

"Do you have anything specific in mind?" I asked.

"I just finished reading a book called, "*Jungle Medicines*". Fascinating stuff. Some very marketable drugs have been discovered in the Amazon and other jungle locations."

"Before we go any further, I'd like to give these ideas some thought," I said.

"Take your time, just not too much," Mel laughed.

"Is there some sort of an agreement you have with the Belize government that we should talk about?" I asked.

"We can follow up on that later. Tomorrow, I'm heading back to the site. From now on, I'll be staying there to keep an eye on the work," Mel said. "Let's talk again in a day or two. In the meantime, we'll both think of what the next steps might be. Why don't you put together a wish list of items for the lab?

Then we can talk again."

We shook hands and as I walked back to my room, I couldn't help but wonder what he meant by his earlier comment about the karmic debt to the people of Belize.

That night, I lay staring at the ceiling fan circling overhead. Part of me wondered if this was a way to fund the things that were important, a way to preserve Don Rodrigo's legacy and a way to hold on to some of the healing secrets that would disappear with his passing. Another part of me asked if I might make some of the money I needed to buy a farm.

Four

The sign on the door read 'community meeting'. Peeking inside, I was surprised to see Mel at the podium next to James. The audience was a mix of farmers in work clothes, some local people, tour guides from a travel agency and even a few lodge guests, like me.

Mel took the microphone with casual assurance. "First, I want to thank James, the owner of this fantastic Seven Sisters Lodge, for giving me the opportunity to say a few words before your community meeting today. Like some of you, I'm a newcomer to Belize, but I wanted to tell you how excited I am to be here. I see a few familiar faces, some of the small business owners I've been working with on my project, but I also appreciate the chance to meet those of you who I like to think of as the original inhabitants of this beautiful land, the Maya people.

I was fortunate to receive an economic development grant from the government of Belize. Since the goal of that grant is to create jobs for people, I hope to be working with many of you in the future. But first let me tell you a little about myself. My name is Mel Powers.

I've gotten a lot of press in my time. Stories just seem to latch on to me and follow me around. I'm just that kind of guy. I've been called an idea man. Believe it or not, I worked my way through college selling bibles door to door. It turns out that I was always good at marketing, technology too. Made use of both. My goal was to provide consumers with their heart's desire. I achieved it using the internet and electronic delivery. In the process I became pretty successful.

I sold my first million software packages and after that I was a hot tech ticket. The Wall Street Journal did a story about me. If you read the news about me, you would have thought I was having the best time ever. But I couldn't take it. The stress was non-stop. My brain was screaming. It was time for me to get out and I did.

Once I sold my company, I was sort of at loose ends. For most of my life, I've been a real nuts and bolts kind of guy. But I needed a change. So, to slow myself down, I learned to meditate. That led me to seek answers in the world of spirituality. A lot of people just couldn't believe I'd turned a corner, moving away from the fast track. But what I really wanted was to find a way to make a difference in people's lives.

I moved to the desert, got hooked up with a spiritual teacher, some might call him a guru. Together we had the idea to create a healing center there, a place for people to come and recharge, even see a different way of life. I called it my desert retreat. And for a while, things there were great, until they weren't.

A guy had an accident on the property, fell off a hang glider. He was pretty severely injured. Wasn't my fault, but, of course, he wanted to sue me. Right after that my lawyer advised me to lay low. To get out of sight, I just closed the whole place down. How did I get to Belize? Like many people, it wasn't even on my radar until a couple years ago. I was talking to a guy sitting next to me on a plane to Florida. He'd just got back from making a deal and he was on his way to Belize to look for some property. Said the corporate tax situation was sweet, and the legal oversight was relaxed. Not much regulation on the banking structure. When he asked me if I was interested, I said,

Are you kidding me? That's my kind of place.

Not to get ahead of myself but I've heard some pretty amazing things about the native healers. Now that I'm here, I want to connect with some of the traditional wisdom of the local people. I want to explore the rainforest, learn more about the plant life and find ways that it can benefit mankind. I want to turn over a new leaf, if you will. I'm setting up a foundation. You know Bill Gates is kind of a hero of mine. I'd like to follow in his footsteps. Any questions?"

Five

A few hands popped up and once he'd answered questions about jobs, Mel stepped away from the mic. A smattering of applause and some confused looks by the local people followed his progress toward the back of the room. Next on the agenda, James introduced a young environmentalist who warned of groups crossing the border from Guatemala to poach endangered animals. Other groups were illegally harvesting mahogany and other rare woods on lands designated by the government for the Maya.

Local farmers had tales to tell. They'd seen large swaths of woodlands devastated, and truckloads of logs heading out of the forest. James asked for volunteers to act as eyes and ears and report any illegal activity on the roads leading into and out of the forest. And he offered a reward to anyone who could provide information on the names or license plates of the trespassers.

As the meeting continued, Mel's face registered boredom. Checking the room, he caught me watching him and gave me the high sign. He made for the door, motioning for me to follow him outside. Since our previous meeting. I'd given some thought to boundaries of our partnership, but I still hadn't gotten my head around the logistics of the situation. In an offhand comment, Mel had suggested that if I were interested, he had room for me. If I wanted a place to stay, I could bunk in staff quarters at the compound. At first glance, that might make some sense. Getting around in Belize is rough at best. There were few taxis, no buses; the nearest car rental agency was thirty miles away. But while I had transportation issues, I wanted to keep my independence.

When I talked to my father, he gave that idea a big thumbs down. "Best to stay at the lodge where you feel safe." That's fine to say. With Belize a world away, he wouldn't realize that even though there was only a few miles between the lodge and Mel's compound, I wasn't about to walk. I had to laugh when he offered to FedEx me a bicycle. "Ok," I said, not sure he really meant it.

"You want to finish up the work as fast as you can," Dad said. "You need to realize thatDon Rodrigo won't be around forever."

I held my tongue. I didn't have the guts to tell him of my hopes to stay on in Belize for as long as I could, Don Rodrigo or no. I was afraid that if I revealed my plan, Dad would be on the first flight out of Chicago, hoping to convince me to come home.

"Will this guy give you approval to hire some help?"

I hadn't thought about that. As I turned it over in my head, it felt like the solution I'd been looking for. I could continue my work on the healing plants and best of all, I'd have an ally, someone to watch my back.

Outside the meeting room, Mel and I found chairs in the lobby. I'd written up a rough list of ideas and it seemed like a good time to sound him out on them. Mel was in manic mode as he looked at what I'd written. "Carrie, glad to see you going at this like a business. Here's what I've been thinking, we share profits in any venture. We'll come up the numbers later but, in the meantime, you'll have a budget and a monthly stipend."

He scribbled numbers on my paperwork, and I had to admit

the money he was offering was more generous than anything I'd expected. "I didn't think much about you hiring an assistant, but it makes sense. If it helps us get from Point A to Point B, well, let's go for it."

"I might not have mentioned it before, but the first project should focus on antibiotics. That would be Job One," Mel said. "What do you say to that?"

That sounded exciting. I'd been thinking for a long time about the anti-bacterial properties of the bark of the Ceiba tree. I'd watched Don Rodrigo use it in a variety of ways. Now, with luck, I hoped I would be able to test it under more controlled conditions. This project would give me the freedom to pursue my theory and see where it went.

Mel held out his hand and we shook. I felt a sense of exhilaration and promise mixed with a twinge of fear.

Now where the hell can I find someone who could help me?

Julio's face popped into my head. *Yes, my assistant needs to be someone who knows the way around the rainforest.* While Don Rodrigo was hopeful that he would carry on the traditions of the people but, Julio lived in the modern world of Belize and in that world, you needed cash. I knew he needed a job and I felt I could trust him.

I'd often heard the old man caution his nephew against the lure of easy money to be made on the streets. He, too, had heard of the steady stream of drug traffic coming in from across the border. The money flowed freely but the price was high.

Now I could offer an alternative. Julio would still have time to study with his uncle and he'd have money to live on.

After Mel left, I went looking for James and spotted him coming out of the kitchen. Meeting over, he was in one of his many other roles. Instead of the community organizer nattily dressed in bush jacket and sharply pressed shorts, he was now a kitchen worker in a white t-shirt and scruffy jeans, towel tied around his waist.

As he backed his way out of the kitchen juggling a tray of stacked glassware. I ran to hold the door for him. "Need help?" I asked. "I did my share of busing tables in college."

Red-faced from exertion, he shot me a look of gratitude. "Thanks for the offer. I think Gloria and I can handle tonight's dinner. Most of the tourists left this morning on the bus. So, it'll be slow tonight."

"You deserve a break." I said. "That was quite a meeting. I'm sorry that I missed the end of the discussion about the loggers."

"The environmentalist who spoke wants to set up what he's calling a Ranger Corp to patrol the roads to Guatemala."

"Isn't that something the police should do?" I asked.

"I hate to say it, but the local police have no funding to protect those land rights. Even if they did, I doubt they'd take much action to stop the loggers and poachers. It can be dangerous and to be honest, they don't see it as their job. More people are needed to watch and report what they see."

"I'll keep my eyes open for anything suspicious."

"How are you making out?" James asked. "I saw you and Mel with your heads together earlier. What's happening with you?"

"I accepted an offer that Mel made. So, I'll be working with him on one of the projects he's got funding for. If things go well, I hope to be here in Belize for quite some time. But to be honest, I'm really torn. I'm still worried about Don Rodrigo. And I don't know how he's doing. I'd like to try to get over there. Do you know anyone who might be able to give me a lift?"

"Can't do it tonight. How does tomorrow morning sound?"

The next morning, I woke before sunrise, with a plan in my head. I couldn't blame my wakefulness on a lack of comfort. My room at the lodge was all I could wish for. A terra cotta tile floor shone cleanly underfoot. Crisply laundered bed linens covered a mattress that felt springy to the touch. No creatures crawled around the tiny bathroom. It felt luxurious compared to what I'd been used to at the farm.

No longer able to stay in bed, I dressed, splashed cold water on my face, and stepped outside. A light breeze played across my tiny balcony bringing with it a whiff of moist vegetation. I heard wings flapping overhead. Following the sound with my eyes, I watched as a long-necked heron dropped into the water. Seconds later, it was perched on a rock, gobbling a scaly, wiggling meal.

The sun rose, burning off the mist that enveloped the foliage. As I made my way down the path that led to the main building, the jungle came alive. A howler monkey swung through the trees, while a raucous trio of macaws perched on a bench.

In the dining room, the staff was setting up for breakfast. I was more than ready for the cup of strong coffee a waiter poured for me. No sooner had I put down my empty cup, than James appeared, dangling his keys in front of my nose.

"Ready?" he asked. I nodded and he steered me to where his jeep stood under a tree. "Let's go find Don Rodrigo," he said.

Being away from the farm was difficult. Though it had only been a few days, I was anxious as a child looking forward to seeing my mentor again. I wondered if Josefina was still spending most of her time digging around, looking for money that wasn't there? And who was tending the vegetable garden?

As we bounced along over the rutted one-lane dirt road, James asked, "Have you heard anything from the old man since you left?"

I shook my head. "It wasn't like him to stay away from one of your meetings. I was surprised that he wasn't there. You know how he loves to be with people."

"He usually depends on the local grapevine to let him know what's going on." James said.

"You know there's no landline at the farm and of course, he would never hear of having a cell phone. He barely acknowledges the existence of television or radio. And he wasn't doing well when I left. That's why I'm so anxious to see him."

We pulled up the hill and into the farmyard. All was as I left it. Chickens scratched in the dirt. In their enclosure, the pigs stuck their snouts through the fence posts in hopes of a meal. At the sight of two marauding goats in the vegetable plot eating green, unripe ears of corn off the stalks, I bolted from the jeep, running to chase them out of the garden.

Don Rodrigo's chair on the small porch was empty. At the

sound of wheels on gravel, Josefina came out of the house. When James waved a greeting, her response was a blank look.

Ignoring the sour welcome, I introduced James. "Josefina, good to see you," I fibbed. "James wanted to stop and say hello to your grandfather? Is he here?"

"He is not here. He and Julio went to the forest early. I don't know when they'll come back."

Before she could say more, the two men emerged from the brush as though they had been conjured up. Slowly, Don Rodrigo made his way up the path, with the help of a walking stick. Towering over his uncle, Julio, young, strong, and smiling, carried a large cloth bag that bulged with leaves and plant material.

As James walked down the hill to greet his old friend, Don Rodrigo's eyes lit up. "*Bien venidos*. Welcome, my friends." The old man's weathered face filled with good humor.

James helped the healer up the few porch steps. "It's hot, you must be tired. But don't worry. I have something to revive you," he said.

From the back of the jeep, James produced a small cooler. Pulling bottles of the local brew from the melting ice, he popped off the lid before placing it in the old man's hand. When James offered the second bottle to Julio, Josefina, not to be ignored, held out her hand for one.

"*Lo siento, Señora,*" James said. "Where are my manners." He opened more bottles, passing one first to Josefina, then to me.

We all toasted, "*Buena salud Don Rodrigo!*" And for a few moments, it felt like a homecoming with my heart warm in my chest. But as we enjoyed the drinks, I noticed something missing, "Julio where's your car?"

"I loaned it to my cousin, Ramon. He went to pick up a couple of Josefina's grandkids in San Ignacio. They'll be here for a while. They're coming in on the bus."

"But he'll be back with the car today?" I asked.

Julio nodded.

"I remembered that you were looking for work."

"Yes, I am still looking."

"That's good because I need a driver, someone with a car who can drive me to the place where I'm working. I can pay you for your time and of course, gas. But that's not all. I also need an assistant for about twenty hours a week to help me gather herbs and do some work in the lab. That would still give you time to work with Don Rodrigo. Does that sound like something you might be interested in?"

"Yes," Julio nodded, giving the idea a vigorous thumbs up. "I can do both."

Looking on, Josefina fumed. She spoke to Julio in a rapid-fire tongue that I took to be Mayan. He fired back and shook his head.

Julio turned away from Josefina. "When shall I start?"

"How does tomorrow sound? Can you pick me up at the lodge at 7:30? Do you have a cell phone?"

Julio looked a little shame faced. "*Sí.*"

"I'm glad you have one but I'm going to give you another one that's just for the two of us to use. When you pick me up tomorrow, we can go into town and buy it."

Six

"Carrie, Carrie." A female voice called. It was Gabrielle. Mel's what? His housekeeper, live-in girlfriend? What the arrangement was, I couldn't be sure.

"Carrie, are you hungry? I brought you coffee and something to eat. Let me in."

"Oh, sorry. I must have locked the door by mistake."

Gabrielle came in balancing a tray on her slender hip, her glossy dark hair swept over one eye. "Here's some eggs and fruit. Do you like tortillas?"

The coffee smelled delicious. My last meal had been hours ago. Even then it was just some crackers and little else.

"God bless you. I'm starving."

"Oh, no problem. I like to do it. I love to cook. Mel doesn't eat much and I'm not about to do the cooking for those guys." She motioned with her head toward the courtyard where Mel's security detail played a loud game of kick ball. "Every once in a while, I'm willing to cook them up a big pot of rice and beans but they can fend for themselves."

Gabrielle looked for a place to put her tray. I moved the laptop out of the way, and we sat down. There were two cups on the tray along with three boiled eggs, sliced melon and best of all, the homemade tortillas. I dug in.

"Have you known Mel long?" I asked.

"Not too long. We met when he was staying at the hotel on San Pedro Caye. He took a boat over from the airport. I was working at the restaurant there. You know you meet a lot of crazy characters here in Belize, but I never met anyone like him before." Her eyes shone with admiration.

I had to agree. "Mel is one of a kind."

"Try the tortillas," she said. "They're still warm."

I helped myself. "Is Belize your home? Were you born here?"

"No, I came here with my family. From Honduras. I was a kid. There was so much violence and corruption at home. Not as bad as it is now, but my father wanted to get away. My uncle was the leader of the village. An electric company bought up some land near our village. They wanted to build a dam and divert the water from the river. If that happened, we would have no water for our crops. The company and the government wanted my uncle to convince the people of the village to agree to it, to be part of it. But he said no. Then one day, a motorcycle pulled up next to his car and they shot him. The police would do nothing.

"My father decided that it was time to leave. And it was good that we did. Soon after that, my uncle's home was burned, and our house was next to it. Once that happened there was no reason to stay. It was sad to leave all our cousins and all the people in our village. Belize was much more peaceful in those days. So, we came here. My father got some work as a carpenter. He was away a lot and my mother worked as a maid at the hotel. My brothers and I raised ourselves as best we could."

She sipped her coffee. "My parents worked hard. They did

their best. Got citizenship. Back then if you became a Belizean citizen you got fifty acres and a machete."

"Do you plan to stay here with Mel?" I asked.

"My dream is to go to America." She looked wistful. "And Mel says he will take me there someday."

At the sound of Mel's voice outside, she picked up the empty cups. "I better go. Oh, but one more thing. Don't let the talk about the gangs frighten you."

"Gangs? What gangs?"

"The gangs think that Mel is trying to take over their action. But he is not interested in that. He told me so many times." She made for the door.

Mel called her name. "Gabrielle, I'm going out for a while. Close the gate behind us and keep your eye on the cameras." He jumped into his jeep. The gate opened and he and his security detail sped away.

Commotion outside. Dogs barked and growled. What was it this time? Excited by the least activity, they would run toward the road. A truck backfired. I looked out. Gabrielle waved the remote from the main house to open the gate. A yellow DHL truck lumbered its way into the compound. Was my delivery here? Excited and anxious, I went to check

The driver squinted at me, then at his clipboard. "You Carrie Mullen?"

I nodded.

"You got seven boxes from the U. S." He didn't look impressed as he held out the receipt for me to sign

"I guess DHL really is a global company, like they say," I joked hoping to make conversation. We didn't get too many outsiders around here.

He pulled the boxes off the truck but showed no inclination

to take them any further. No use looking for some help. It was just me and the dogs. Once I offered him a couple Belize dollars the driver moved the boxes near the steps to the lab. While I was busy reading the label on the top box, he got in the truck and drove out. The gate clanked shut.

Birds scattered as a strong wind rustled leaves overhead. Rainy season was on the way and chances were good it could rain that night. I called Julio and asked if he could come over and help me get the equipment inside. He'd dropped me off this morning, but this would be his first time inside the compound. Nervously, I waited at the gate ready to let him in. I hoped it would give me a chance to introduce him to Mel.

As Julio pulled in next to where I stood, the dogs came on snarling. Opening the car door, the young man's dark head bent low as he murmured to the dogs. When they quietly backed away, Julio got out unfazed.

I was impressed. "They scare most visitors. How did you know how to handle them?"

"Show no fear," he said. "And speak softly. Their tails were wagging so I knew they wouldn't attack."

Down by the stream, the frogs bellowed. Thunder clouds pushed against the horizon and fat drops of rain were starting to fall. Julio moved quickly to get the boxes inside. "Do you want to unpack them?" he asked.

I opened a case of petri dishes. "They can wait. How is your uncle?" "He wants to come visit you. He wants to see where you are working."

"Thank you for telling me. More than anything, I want him to approve of what I'm doing." Still, I hesitated. "Before I invite him, let me make sure that Mel is OK with that, it might be better to wait."

What am I doing? How did I let myself get so sidetracked?

Not for the first time, the words of Jeff, my undergraduate mentor echoed in my brain.

"Our job is to bridge the gap between the wisdom of the traditional healers and modern medical techniques." How could I forget? Just like Jeff, I wanted to help share this wisdom. It was why I'd come to Belize.

Julio and I ran through the rain to the main house. "Hello," I called, peeking in.

"Come on back," Gabrielle yelled. "In the kitchen."

I introduced Julio and once they'd traded hellos, Gabrielle offered us something cold to drink. Julio quickly accepted and while neither of them said much, a spark seemed to connect the two. As their eyes met, Gabrielle curled a lock of dark hair behind an ear. Julio stood a little straighter. It was probably best that Mel wasn't around to see that. And what about me? *Is the sting in my chest jealousy?*

The rain stopped as suddenly as it had started, and the sun came out. And I decided it was a good time to hustle my young helper out of the kitchen. Too late. As we made for the back door, Mel came in the front bellowing for Gabrielle.

"Gabrielle, whose car is that? I told you to keep an eye on things."

Gabrielle looked over to where Julio and I hovered on the perimeter.

I stepped up. "Oh, sorry, Mel. The car belongs to Julio."

"And who's he?" Mel asked, pointing.

"That's Julio"

"Who?"

"My new assistant, remember?" I offered. "You might have seen him the other day when he dropped me off."

Mel growled an inaudible response.

"I'm the one that opened the gate," I said. "I needed help and Julio came over to give me a hand. He was just about to leave, but I was hoping I'd have a chance to introduce him to you."

"Pleased to meet you, *Señor* Mel." Julio held out his hand.

Suddenly, two gunshots ripped through the moist afternoon air. The dogs went crazy and the guard supervisor ran in. "*Señor, Señor* Mel. Come quick. Trouble outside."

Mel ran out and Gabrielle dove under the table, clutching her phone. My intuition told me to lock myself in the bathroom and on instinct, I dragged Julio in with me. The close quarters had us almost belly to belly. I couldn't help looking into his brown eyes and nervously, we smiled at each other. A flush rose to my face, and I stepped back as far as the tiny space would let me. Standing on tiptoe, I peered through the one small windowpane. I couldn't see anything, but the noise level continued to grow with more yelling, dogs barking. Then all was quiet.

"Why don't you take a look?" I said to Julio. He had a good four or five inches on me. He moved to the window. "I see Mel and one of his security guys dragging the young American guard, I heard them call him Ronnie. They threw him in the storage shed and locked him in from the outside."

An hour later, the police gang unit, carrying guns and dressed in camo, arrived in their pickup. Mel trotted a bruised and disoriented Ronnie out to face the authorities. "Just a minor misunderstanding," Mel said. "No problem."

After a tense discussion, Mel promised a contribution to the municipal coffers. Soon, our local law enforcement departed with a full bottle of whiskey, a gift for the head cop. As the dust of their tires faded, Mel stood in the middle of the courtyard. When he fired three shots in the air, I let out a scream. "Don't worry," Gabrielle said. "It's his signal for everyone to gather outside." We all straggled out.

I could tell he was pissed. "Dammit, Gabrielle. I told you never to call those idiots."

"So sorry, Mel. I got scared when I heard shooting."

The guards brought Ronnie over to face Mel.

"Ronnie, what the fuck? Are you trying to cause me trouble?"

"A truck went by. Somebody threw something," Ronnie said, looking pale and shaken. "Whatever it was hit the fence. I took it for a grenade or a bomb. Like in Ramallah. I went to code red. My bad."

Mel's face registered irritation. Looking around, he spotted Julio. "OK, Mr. New Assistant, you go check and see what hit the fence over there."

Julio came back some minutes later carrying a large brown husk. "*Señor* I only found this. A rotten coconut. Somebody must have thrown it out when they went by."

Obviously not OK, I thought. "Mel, that was a little scary," I said. "What if next time, Ronnie thinks you or me or Gabrielle are the enemy? Then what?"

Julio whispered to me. "Ronnie. I think he is sick with the susto."

"Sick with what?" Mel overheard. "What's susto?"

"It's the fear." Julio said with conviction. "Was he in the war?" Ronnie must have heard. "Yeah, I did a tour in Iraq. More than one."

"You said you were OK," Mel said.

Ronnie hung his head again.

Julio turned to me. "If Don Rodrigo were here, he could help him with the susto."

Mel changed gears. Instead of carrying on with his rant, he turned a calm visage to the perpetrator. "Ronnie, my friend, you are a person we want to help. You're suffering flashbacks. Go inside with Gabrielle." He turned to her, "Honey, give him some whiskey and something to eat."

Gabrielle looked askance but she followed orders and led Ronnie to the house. The other two guards followed in hopes of getting in on the meal plan. Mel shrugged his shoulders and put his gun on safety. He turned to Julio. "If Ronnie needs help, why not bring your Don Rodrigo over. Maybe he can do something for him. Whaddya say?"

Seven

I'd been excited after the first delivery for the lab. Seeing the test tubes, petri dishes and other familiar gear somehow made this whole new endeavor more real. My anticipation grew as I waited for the "big stuff", the mechanical equipment. The refrigeration unit, the drying cabinets, burners, scales and the centrifuge were all critical for the botanical research I hoped to embark on. In graduate school I'd often made use of these tools, but since then, I'd spent my time in the jungles of Belize. With Don Rodrigo, my methods were limited to gathering herbs in the forest, hanging them up to dry in the barn and grinding them with a mortar and pestle, or on a stone slab. It had all been extremely low tech. Working in an actual lab again would be an adjustment.

Tracking notices began to show up on my computer screen, and I knew that the big equipment was on its way. Days later, a message confirmed that the shipment had arrived at the Belize

City airport. With Mel's remote compound miles away, in an area with bad roads, delivery could still be days away. Maybe that was a good thing. It would buy some time to get everything else in place.

True to his word, Mel had provided access to his credit card along with the promised budget that allowed me to order high end equipment. Beyond that he wasn't terribly interested in the nuts-and-bolts phase of getting the project up and running. When he did stick his head in the lab, his chief communication was that he wanted things to move fast.

As I would come to learn, his enthusiasms ran from hot to cold and they were many. When no one else was around he might use me as a sounding board for his endlessly churning ideas. Some things he came up with made sense, such as buying the unused field across from his property to create a landing pad. More often, though, these crazy whims were best forgotten the next day and to those, I would just nod silently.

Constantly in motion, Mel spent a good deal of time away from the compound. On several occasions, he'd gone to the capital to meet with the Minister of Economic Development, spending time networking with government officials he hoped might be helpful in supporting his plans. That was fine with me. Julio and I made good use of the quiet days, preparing the space before the equipment arrived.

Having Julio's help felt like a blessing. My guess was that he'd never seen the inside of a high school classroom or a textbook, let alone a science laboratory. But lucky for me, he had a natural sense of how things worked and how they fit together. He mentioned previous jobs doing construction and he certainly knew his way around a toolbox. Making good use of the hammers, wrenches and whatnot he kept in the trunk of his car, he rewired the generator, installed outlets and connected the sink, the faucets and water pipes joined to the outside water line.

I did my part, painting walls and shelves and doing some minor carpentry. During a break, I might take out my notes, collected during my time in the forest with Don Rodrigo. My goal was to convert lists, observations, and hastily scribbled notations into a working strategy for extracting medicinal properties from various jungle plants. Things were coming together.

Working around the clock, Julio and I spent all our daylight hours in the lab. Often, he'd pick me up at first light, as the birds chirped a welcome to the new day. We'd arrive at the compound just as the sun came up. At midday, Gabrielle might stop by with some sandwiches and cool drinks. Although he didn't say much, I noticed that Julio perked up on these occasions. Feeling a little on edge, I tried never to leave the two of them alone.

I almost felt a kinship with Gabrielle. The two of us needed Mel's support, financial or otherwise to sustain our current situations. I didn't want to be part of anything that would mess that up.

Dusk comes on fast and once the light began to fade; we were ready to call it quits. Julio would drop me at the lodge before he made the drive to San Ignacio, the town he now called home. Even though his rented room was above a noisy café, he was proud and happy to have a place of his own.

Back in my cabin at the lodge, I'd fight the urge to stretch out across the bed. If I managed to stay upright and awake, I might relax with a welcome shower and a refreshing spritz of cologne. On those evenings, I rewarded myself with a stroll through the garden on my way to dinner and, maybe, a cocktail in the bar.

Outside my room, flickering torches illuminated each of the small thatch-roofed guest bungalows that clustered like a small village around the lodge grounds. Flowering hibiscus lined a gravel path that led to the main building that housed the dining rooms, snack bar, gift shops, kitchens and staff quarters.

In the evening quiet, I breathed in the sweet scents of the flowering allspice bushes. I shared the space with a couple walking by, their arms entwined. Seeing them triggered a stab of loneliness that went right to my core. Before I could examine those feelings further, I was distracted by the merry laughter of two young women, one fair-haired, one dark and one very tall young man, all three dressed in shorts and hiking boots. I took them for students and for a moment, I saw myself, in the not-so-distant past, reflected in their carefree posture. They waved a "Hello" as they passed, continuing on their way and I tagged along keeping a few yards behind, enjoying the sound of their banter.

I trailed them to the open-air bar on the porch, watching as they found a table. One of the young women, a sturdy-looking blond, her face bright with sunburn, asked the waiter for a drink suggestion.

"You might want to try our house specialty," he said. "It's called the Belize Sunrise."

"That sounds good. What's in it?"

"It's rum, pineapple juice and syrup from the agave plant."

"Guess I'll try it," she said.

"It's delicious," I piped up. "You won't be disappointed. May I treat you and your friends?" At that moment I was eager to hear more of their cheerful teasing, something sorely missing from my life.

Happily, they agreed, and I gave the bartender my room number. They invited me to join them at their table, and the three introduced themselves as graduate students in archaeology at the University of New Mexico. They'd arrived at the lodge filled with plans to visit the Maya sites nearby. "We came with the idea that we would spend most of our time visiting the ruins like Caracol but there are so many things to see that we haven't gotten there yet," the young man said.

Their day had been spent with a diving excursion to the Blue

Hole, one of the country's major tourist attractions. Called the biggest sinkhole in the world, the Blue Hole is filled with sparkling clear fresh water and surrounded by caves and steep cliffs. The young students claimed it had the best snorkeling ever.

"I've heard that the Blue Hole is pretty deep, maybe twenty-five feet at some spots. You guys must be good snorkelers. I wouldn't expect you'd get much diving practice in New Mexico."

They laughed. Margo, the dark-haired young woman pointed to their clean-cut male companion. "Tell her, Josh."

"Yeah, we're all originally from California," he said. "I'm from Malibu. I was a real surfer dude back in the day."

"Yeah, Josh. That was before you let me cut your hair," said the blond. Her name was Ellen. They laughed some more.

The students were enthusiastic travelers. In love with Belize, they were eager to share their experiences. Their next day's excursion was to be a visit to Barton Creek, a remote labyrinth of caves, once used as an ancient Maya burial site. It could only be reached by boat. As they chattered on about what they'd seen already and other places they hoped to visit, I was more than a little surprised when they mentioned the herb farm in the nearby village of San Mateo. Ellen spoke up, "We heard it's the home of a famous shaman, Don Rodrigo. Have you heard of him?"

I caught my breath. "Yes, I know him well. He truly is a local treasure." They were a rapt audience as I told them of my college dreams and how I came to be in Belize. Once they finished peppering me with questions, I asked, "How did you guys hear of Don Rodrigo?"

"We only heard about him last night. We had a great time talking to the lodge owner. He's a real Belize pioneer." The young man pointed to James who was tending bar. "He's a big- time environmentalist, pretty much into everything that goes on around here. Been here for years. In fact, he told us he was here when the Barton Creek caves were rediscovered. Of course, as he says, they were never really lost. The local people knew the burial sites were here all along. They just didn't bother to tell the gringos. Can't say you could blame them."

"Yes, Belize keeps its secrets," I said. "When you see a beautiful place like the Seven Sisters Lodge, it's hard to believe that until maybe twenty or thirty years ago, tourists rarely came to Belize." I said. "It was all jungle and farmland. There were very few roads, even fewer hotels. Now there are tons of tourists every year and more coming all the time."

Margo raised her drink. "To Belize!" she laughed. We clinked glasses.

Cocktail time finished; the students announced plans to grab sandwiches from the snack bar. They were turning in early to be up at first light for the trip to Barton Creek. I hoped I would see them again.

Many things had changed in the years since James and Gloria opened the doors of the Seven Sisters Lodge. Somehow, I got the impression they weren't totally thrilled with all the new tourist flavored developments springing up around the countryside. They knew that more expansion was inevitable. If you are in the tourist business, you can't avoid new people coming into the area and deciding that they want a little piece of this heaven for themselves. But the lodge owners were most concerned that their piece of paradise was threatened, not by tourism, but by outside corporate interests. They believed that companies, in search of oil or mineral reserves for exploitation, were more of a danger.

Sometimes, if it was a slow night, and there were just a few guests, the owners would drift from table to table, chatting with their customers and they were fun company. But tonight, it looked like all the rooms at the lodge were full. The room took on a festive air as glasses clinked and a couple of musicians near the bar began playing something with a Latin flavor.

Maybe I should tell Julio about the musicians. He'd mentioned how much he loved playing guitar at a local spot on Saturday nights "Now that I got over my stage fright, I'm looking for gigs," he said.

The dining room was filling up. A hostess motioned me to a table. Nudged by hunger pangs, I was ready to order, I studied the Seven Sisters menu, a mix of European and Latin dishes. Mouth-watering fragrances drifted by as the waiters rushed plates from the kitchen, serving them with a European flourish. Once I'd placed my order for a pasta dish, I told the waiter I'd be right back. On my way to the restroom, I noticed a wall of framed photos and newspaper clippings along the corridor. One large article drew my attention with headlines that read, **Mayan Ranger Corps to Protect Indigenous Land**.

Despite efforts by local activists, it seemed they were almost too late. New licenses were being granted by the government and forests were being cleared in direct violation of previous guarantees. With the establishment of the Ranger Corps, scores of volunteers, Maya and Anglo alike pledged time and money to protect against these illegal incursions onto indigenous land. The article described recent protests against mineral and logging rights granted to foreign companies on land preserves the Belize government once guaranteed to the Maya. Below was a photo of James, tall, pale-skinned, and white-haired, towering over a group of shorter, dark- haired indigenous people.

As I studied the article, Gloria walked by, balancing a tray on her hip. "That's my James," she said pointing. "We're so proud of the work he's done."

"This is quite a testimonial, isn't it? I can see why you would be."

Sweeping a lock of fair hair off her forehead, Gloria turned back toward the dining room. "These days, I still spend most of my time managing the lodge while James works with the Maya Rangers that patrol the area. But they have to do it," she said, blue eyes blazing." Unfortunately, you really can't count on the local police to do much."

Considering recent events at Mel's compound, I had to agree. From what I'd seen, the police, more than anything, were open to a payoff. But I kept mum.

"Scoundrels from outside feel free to come in, hack through forest and steal whatever they want. They think no one is watching," Gloria said. "But they're wrong. Someone is watching."

Eight

Dark clouds overhead foretold the approach of rain. Yet a strong wind rattling the palm fronds did little to cool the muggy air. It was delivery day, and Julio and I had been waiting since morning for the yellow DHL truck to appear, bringing the final load of lab equipment. According to the invoices in my hand there should be eight boxes, and all of them sure to be heavy. It was mid-afternoon before the gate clanked open. The dogs let us know that the truck had arrived. As they swarmed yapping around the vehicle, the driver made no move to get out and I couldn't blame him. Instead, he just handed me his clipboard through the passenger side window. While I checked my paperwork against his list, I could hear Julio negotiating with the driver in Spanish. He looked frustrated.

"What's up?" I asked.

"He's afraid of the dogs," Julio said. Some small bills changed hands. "He don't want to get out of the truck." It seemed to be the custom of the country; Belize truckers did not understand the concept of free delivery. Julio herded the dogs back to their pen, and only then did the guy emerge from behind the wheel. He produced his hand truck, but instead of doing his job, he watched us wrestle the load up the steps.

"Do you believe this guy?" I said.

Julio shrugged. As the trucker leaned against the van for a smoke break, Julio and I sweated the boxes inside. By the time we finished the driver had packed up his hand truck and had already driven out the gate. Soon after, thunder and lightning brought on a downpour.

"I hope you get stuck in a mud rut." I muttered under my breath.

Next day, with the lab set up and the equipment in place, Mel paid a visit. His low whistle and the high five he offered showed approval. "Let's show off what we've accomplished here," he said.

"What did you have in mind?" I asked.

Mel shrugged.

I knew Don Rodrigo wanted to visit, to see where Julio and I would be working. When I asked if it would be OK for Julio to bring his uncle, he was all for it. "Yeah, tell him to bring the old man," Mel said. "He sounds like quite a character and I like characters."

Within minutes, Mel began to think that having Don Rodrigo visit was his idea. Once an idea entered his brain it might continue to percolate until the next bright object distracted him. "Let's get a film crew in here," he said. "How about we do a ribbon-cutting? This lab should be a key part of that development grant I got from the government. If your friend, Don Rodrigo is here, he'll add some local color. Besides, they'll see we're involving the indigenous people."

He handed me a card. It had the raised logo of the Belizean government and a name and title to go along with it. "Give this guy a call. Be sure to use my name. Tell him we want the cameras back. If there's a problem, let me know."

I followed orders, arranging for an afternoon visit by a TV film crew a few days ahead. Mel liked the plan. With luck, Don

Rodrigo would be here with Julio and the cameras would record the event for Belize Channel Four television. Until then I would spend my time polishing the newly arrived refrigeration equipment, arranging beakers on the shelves, and thinking of possible answers to any questions that the filmmakers might ask. For a split second I even wondered if I should I try to go to the village and buy some ribbon for a ribbon-cutting ceremony until I talked myself out of it. No way, that's crazy.

On the day of the event, Julio called on my cell to say he and Don Rodrigo were at the gate. They needed someone to let them in "We came early," he said. "My uncle was afraid he'd be too tired later."

"Let me go find Mel," I said. "He's heard so much about Don Rodrigo. He wants to meet him."

At the house, all was quiet, no one around. "Mel, Gabrielle?" I called from the door, not wanting to go farther. A toilet flushed and Mel emerged from a back bedroom, a towel around his middle. I could see Gabrielle beyond the half open door. I turned a blind eye.

"Today's the day. We have company." I reminded him of the purpose of the healer's visit. Mel seemed to have forgotten. He grabbed the intercom, "Ronnie, open the gate. Make sure you keep an eye on the film crew."

"They're not here yet," I said. "Right now, it's just Julio and Don Rodrigo."

"So, you don't need me now," Mel said, sounding relieved. "Once everybody gets here, and everything is set up, let me know."

I nodded agreement. Out front, Ronnie was on "stand by" and the gate was open. When Julio turned the ignition, his beleaguered white sedan bucked and backfired. It was sad to see Ronnie jump and break out in a sweat but, luckily, he kept his hands by his sides. I was thankful there was no holster on his belt.

Julio parked and as they got out, I took Don Rodrigo's hand in both of mine. He smiled warmly. "*Es bueno verte,*" he said. "It is good to see you."

"It is good to see you, too." I relaxed in the comfort of his presence. "Let's go inside." I pointed to the lab.

As they followed behind, I heard Julio and his uncle speaking a few words in the Mayan tongue. Over the years, I'd come to be familiar with the sound, with its many consonants and few vowels, but aside from a few basic expressions, the language was beyond my understanding. Don Rodrigo looked back toward the guard station where Ronnie stood. Were they talking about him? Probably, it was only days before that he'd fired off his gun in a panic.

Inside the lab, Don Rodrigo's eye missed little. He walked around inhaling deeply. "I like to smell the new wood," he said.

"Mel's looking forward to meeting you," I said. "He's busy right now but he'll be here soon."

"Who is Mel?" Don Rodrigo wondered.

"*El jefe*. The boss," Julio said.

He nodded. For a split second, the wry grin I knew so well flickered across his face. The twinkle in his eye revealed a spirit as playful as ever. He poked into boxes and peered in the refrigerator. He stared at the drying unit with a puzzled expression. He took an empty test tube from the rack. He fingered a Bunsen burner not yet connected to a power source. "*Que hace esto?* What does this do?"

"*No se*. I don't know," said Julio.

"*Mi hija*, why are there are no plants here?" His voice sounded worried. "What will you work on?"

"We'll start collecting the plants soon." I brought out my overflowing notebooks. "Do you remember these? I have so many notes written from our time together. I'm still thinking about where to start."

"Start where your heart tells you to start," he said. "You must believe."

Did I believe? Believe in myself? For the first time I wasn't sure.

"Bless you, my friend, I hope your work will give you pleasure." His tone, forgiving as it was, filled me with sadness. The unspoken words were a reminder that our time together had come to an end.

"I hope what I do here in the lab will provide a way for me to stay on in Belize. To continue the work we started together. More than anything, I want to make a database of all the plants, and how you taught me to use them."

He turned to me. *"Bueno,* if you can show the value in these plants, then scientists and doctors will come to respect us. They will listen to us. That will be worth my time." After looking around for a few more minutes, he seemed to lose energy. "I'll just sit for a while," he said. Sinking down on a stool, he closed his eyes and leaned back against the wall. In seconds he drifted off.

Mel entered the lab, spotting Don Rodrigo in the corner, he moved to his side and tapped him lightly on the shoulder. When the old man's eyes blinked open, Mel introduced himself.

Don Rodrigo tried to rise, but Mel protested, "Sit, sit, *Señor.* Here. I'll put this stool over next to you and we can get to know each other." As they sat talking together, the tough-hearted businessman was as gracious as I'd ever seen him.

Gabrielle stuck her head in, and Mel called her over. Don Rodrigo, his usual charming self, bowed over her hand and kissed it. *"Encantado, Señorita."*

Mel gave her a pat on the shoulder. "Gabrielle, how about you and Julio go get us thing to drink?" He turned to Don Rodrigo. "This is a celebration! How about a beer, my friend?"

The old man nodded and smiled. They seemed to be of like mind.

Gabrielle returned quickly with some of the local brew. We each took one. "Here's to new friends and new ventures," Mel said, bowing to Don Rodrigo.

"Salud!"

Mel gulped down his beer and looked around. "Carrie, the lab looks good, but something is missing," he said.

"What do you mean?"

"It needs something to give it a lived-in feel. Like real work is going on. Let's give it a little bit of a pick-me-up."

Oh, no. Not that again.

"Gabrielle. C'mere kiddo." He put his hand on her shoulder.

"Let's help Carrie, our little scientist here."

Little scientist? You bastard.

"Maybe break out some test tubes. Put something in them to make it look authentic."

Authentic? My mouth dropped open. As we'd worked to set up the lab, I'd given Julio a shorthand explanation about scientific experiments and how they must be proven correct by repeating many times. I probably got carried away and when I came out with the word reproducible, the puzzled look on his face told me that I'd gotten ahead of myself. I suspected that all of my blather went right over his head and why wouldn't it. I doubted now, if anything Mel was saying registered with Julio but the relationship I aspired to have with the scientific method, just flew out the window.

Mel handed the girl an empty beaker. "Here, take this and see if there's something in the kitchen, something colorful to put in a test tube."

A few minutes later, Gabrielle was back with a pitcher of bright green liquid. "Kool-Aid," she whispered.

Mel thought it was perfect. "See how smart she is?" He gave the young girl a quick hug. "That's why I keep her around."

Gabrielle wriggled with pleasure at his approval while I fumed.

Oh sure, perfect. What next?

As the three-person television crew arrived in the back of a truck, the compound was quiet. I was glad that Mel had the sense to pen up the dogs and send the rest of his security detail off on an errand. Only Ronnie remained.

While Mel went out to greet the newcomers, he told me to stay in the lab and set up some equipment for the shot. I arranged a couple of flasks and a rack of test tubes. Gabrielle busied herself pouring water into the test tubes and swirling the green Kool-Aid in the flask for effect.

If there was a flashing sign of warning, this was it. Is this a legitimate undertaking or a joke? I don't know what kept me from running screaming into the jungle.

Once the mic was in Mel's face, I knew an hour could pass

while he talked, entranced by the sound of his own voice. Outside, I heard Mel sharing his thoughts on possible endeavors. The basics seemed to have changed from his first recorded conversation. Thank God, this time he didn't mention a cure for cancer.

As he and the camera crew moved into the lab, I was fascinated to hear what he would have to say. "Our plan is to connect with Don Rodrigo here. Of course, he needs no introduction. My dear friend is considered to be one of the most knowledgeable healers in Belize. He can help us make use of the cures of the ancients and repackage them for the modern world."

He picked up the flask and swirled the green Kool-Aid. Turning to the camera, "This is the beginning of what I hope will be the most important work of my life," he said.

"Could you describe for us the project goals?" the filmmaker asked, off-camera. "What do you hope to accomplish for your first project?"

Mel's brow furrowed for a minute. Then without taking a breath, he plowed ahead. "We're developing a new antibiotic."

If my thesis committee professors could see me now, swirling flasks of colored water in front of the camera, they wouldn't believe it. I could barely believe it myself.

With Mel, Don Rodrigo, Gabrielle, Julio, me and the three-person film crew stuffed inside the small lab, it was getting hot and crowded. The woman behind the camera suggested that we move outside so that the crew could finish up and get back to the TV studio before dark. "We'd like to get this edited, maybe show it over the weekend," she said.

Mel herded everyone out. "It's time for our closing ceremony and I asked Don Rodrigo to bless our venture," Mel said.

Walking down the steps outside, the old man pulled a small bundle of dried herbs from his bag. We watched as he lit the plant mixture and held it aloft. As the smoke curled up over the small frame structure, he began a chant, one that I'd heard before, a chant of cleansing. With the camera following in his wake, he circled the exterior walls of the lab. The fragrant smoke drifted upward, fading into the late afternoon breeze.

Blessing completed, the television crew packed and left. But Don Rodrigo was not done. He called over to where Ronnie stood by the gate. "*Mi hijo?*"

Ronnie looked puzzled. He pointed to himself.

"*Si, si, si.*" Don Rodrigo motioned him to follow. "Come, I want to talk to you."

Ronnie walked over hesitantly, but respectfully until the two stood together. They sought shade under a tree, perching on a rough-hewn bench. From where I stood, I couldn't hear what they were saying but after several minutes, Ronnie began to look calmer. The healer placed his brown hand on the bicep of the distressed man. He seemed to be asking permission. When Ronnie nodded, the healer opened the pouch at his waist and took out a pipe and filled it with tobacco. Then he began singing softly, a chant like the call of a nocturnal bird carrying on the breeze. "Uchli, uchli, uchli...Uruba, Uruba, Uruba. Chogue, chogue, chogue."

Ronnie's face went slack. Eyes closed, he sank back motionless, as the old man continued the tobacco ceremony, blowing smoke over Ronnie's head, shoulders, arms and chest. Lowering the pipe, he returned to the chant, singing softly. The energy of the day went quiet and still. The old man sat silent.

Minutes later Ronnie's eyes fluttered open and he looked around sheepishly. Don Rodrigo held Ronnie's wrist as if to check his pulse. As the troubled young man pulled himself to a standing position, he offered the older man his hand and the two of them stood together, speaking quietly for a few minutes longer. As he walked away smiling, Ronnie gave his shoulders a brisk shake as though throwing off a malady.

Mel watched from a distance, a look of wonder on his face.

Nine

After everyone was gone, Mel ran into the lab, eyes wide, excitement coloring his expression. "That's it. That's it! It'll be a complete healing experience. We'll use the whole gestalt."

"Gestalt, what gestalt?" I asked.

"This." He wheeled about in a circle; arms spread wide. "What you see here. The jungle, the plants, the wildlife, the culture and most of all, Don Rodrigo. The shaman will lead us."

Us?

Just like that, Mel's agenda changed. From the antibiotic, it seemed that he'd moved on to making use of the tobacco ceremony and other plant-based traditional remedies known only to Don Rodrigo and other healers.

Next day, I watched Mel, his sincere salesman expression on his face, as he cornered Julio. I knew that look. He was probing the poor guy's brain, shopping for ideas. I heard him tell Julio he would be an important part of the plan. My guess was that he was hoping for an angle on how to coerce Julio and his uncle into working with him. He wanted their help to heal what I heard him call his "wounded warriors."

"Who are the wounded warriors?" Julio looked around, as though they might be hiding in the brush somewhere. He was in a tight spot and I felt guilty for putting him there. But at least, Julio had options. He could disappear into the jungle and there was no way Mel could find him.

"Tell me more about this susto," Mel asked. "How do you heal it?"

I stepped in to save Julio. "Here in Belize, it's a common term used to describe those who've suffered trauma. They can't sleep, they can't eat, they have nightmares. They're anxious, and nervous. Susto has a lot of names. But it means fear."

"PTSD," said Mel.

"Yes, PTSD," I said.

Mel looked at Julio. "How does Don Rodrigo treat it?"

"He uses the tea ceremony," Julio said.

When pressed for more, Julio offered up a sentence or two about the tea ceremony. He'd only seen his uncle perform it a couple of times. As he spoke, the young man's dark eyes scanned the room as though he was looking for a means of escape.

"Didn't you help him with it?" Mel asked.

"No, sorry. I gotta go," Julio stammered and made a quick exit.

Maybe Julio hadn't helped with that ceremony, but I had. During the first few months of my apprenticeship with Don Rodrigo, I had seen him perform the "tea ceremony" as he called it. It wasn't something he did often. Significant preparation was involved. Still, he'd told me that I should experience it myself. I'd been a reluctant participant, but later I was not sorry. After the physical tiredness lessened, a sense of peace descended like I'd rarely known.

"We're going to create a center for healing," Mel said. "For those suffering from PTSD. We'll bring in the wounded warriors, like Ronnie. Who knows, maybe we could even get insurance to pay for it. What do you think?"

I was dumbfounded. But Mel didn't notice.

He grabbed some paper and a pen and started scribbling. "Here's the main house. But what we'll need are some cabins. I want them to look something like a village, like the ones that James built at the lodge."

For a moment, I thought of the small, charming thatched-roof cabin at the lodge where I spent my nights. Then I looked at the paper Mel was waving in front of my face. Something was missing. "What about the lab?" I asked. I didn't see it on the paper. "What about our contract?"

"Don't worry about it. You'll have plenty to do. It will be a whole therapeutic experience. You'll work with Don Rodrigo. Maybe do some other treatments you've learned with him. And you'll still get paid. How does that sound?"

Strangely what he was saying made some sense. Was I comfortable with what Mel was saying? No, but in the crazy world I now inhabited, this sounded better than doing fake experiments using green Kool-Aid. To be honest, I had already spent many nights awake, wondering how I would be able to maintain experimental protocols and scientific standards in the middle of a jungle. *Now maybe I wouldn't have to.*

"How long should it take us to set this thing up?" he asked.

Had I now become his partner in the planning. "There's more to this than putting up a few thatched roof structures. This is a therapeutic endeavor. You are dealing with serious problems, with people's lives. We don't know that Don Rodrigo will agree to be part of the process."

"Ok, but maybe Julio can convince his uncle to help. Get him over here."

"I know that Don Rodrigo wants Julio to become his apprentice and learn all that he can," I said. "Maybe this could be a step toward doing that."

Why did you tell him that? I could have kicked myself.

"I can see it now," Mel daydreamed out loud. "Start small. Just a handful of guys. First day is get acquainted. Sharing stories in a circle, that kind of thing."

"Who would lead the group?" I asked. "Don Rodrigo is not the one for that."

"I will. I'm great at public speaking. Besides, this wouldn't be the first time I've done this retreat thing. I did it back in the States before I came here. And then afterwards, maybe some therapeutic bathing at the waterfalls?" Mel continued.

"Do you mean that beautiful little waterfall downstream?"

"Yeah, that's the one. I don't know who owns it, but we'll find out."

"Or," Mel continued, "a moonlight walk at the Maya ruins at Caracol. Next day, we bring in the old shaman. He does a group healing and that night we do the ceremony, the tea ceremony."

"Which tea is that?" I was testing him now.

"You know, the one with the spirit plants. You brew it up. They drink it and get rid of all the bad karma."

Don Rodrigo, my guide, and teacher was, by my reckoning, closing in on close to ninety-five years. Even if he were to agree to Mel's plan, his physical health would not allow for it.

I had never performed the tea ceremony, but I knew which plants to harvest. I'd seen him prepare the tea and I'd listened closely to the prayers. Julio could learn the chants; he knew the language and I knew the ritual. Don Rodrigo could be trusted to teach us the rest.

"Mel, I see how Ronnie suffers. Maybe there's a way to help him with his PTSD using some other remedies."

"But there are no female shamans."

"You're wrong about that," I said. "They may have a different name, but there are many here in Belize. In fact, I have the knowledge and the belief. We'll take it slow. I can do this, and Julio can help me."

When Julio and I met with Don Rodrigo, we asked many questions. "Your heart must be ready for the *la medicina*," he said. "It is not part of our tradition, but, truly, it can heal."

"How did you first learn of it?" Julio asked.

"Many years ago, I was a young man working in the chicle camps together with *mi padre*. My father befriended a wise man from the south, born in a small village along the *rio Amazona*. When he came to the camps, he taught us many things. We all became close, like family, and he invited us, my father and I, to come visit his home in South America. I had never been on such a boat before, but my father told me to be brave. It was a long journey, and we saw many things along the Amazon River. It was there, that I learned of la medicina."

"Can you tell me what to do to make myself ready?" Julio said.

"It is most important to prepare by cleansing the body."

"You must tell us how."

The first three days of the therapy would be days of healing spent in preparation with fasting, bathing and meditation. No meat, no alcohol. That was a must. This time should be spent quietly in nature, in meditation and prayer. That would be followed by the tobacco ceremony on the next day and finally, the tea ceremony for those who wished to participate.

Mel was on board. "Carrie, I like this plan you've come up with. But, before we try it, how about a little experiment. Let's see if our friend Ronnie will agree to try it. Then if he agrees, let's see where it goes."

Mel called Ronnie over from his post at the gate. Clapping him on the back in a friendly gesture, Mel said, "Ronnie, you are the man. How would you like to be part of an important scientific experiment?"

"Sorry, Boss, not me. When I came back from Iraq, I was homeless, living in a shelter. So, my buddy told me about this place where you could sign up, be part of an experiment and get paid. It sounded easy but they gave me some pills that made me crazy. After that, I swore never again. Sorry, can't do that no more. No experiments for me. Count me out."

"Yeah, that sounds rough, but this will be completely different. You'll be part of a healing ceremony. It'll be a therapeutic experience."

"Therapeutic? Yeah, that's what they called it at the VA hospital when I went there. But that didn't work for me either," Ronnie said.

"But wait," Mel said. "Don't be so quick to shoot this thing down. I swear there's no pills involved. You'll be working with your friend, Don Rodrigo. You trust him, right?"

Ronnie nodded but kept his arms crossed.

"And I want you to keep a record of your thoughts and feelings while it's happening. How does that sound?"

"Like to help out but I barely passed English in high school. And my handwriting sucks."

"How about this," Mel said. "How about if I give you a little recorder and all you have to do is push the button and talk into it. It'll fit right in your shirt pocket. It's about half the size of a pack of smokes."

Ronnie looked skeptical.

"And you'll get paid."

Later, Ronnie turned up at the door of the lab. "Carrie, let me ask you something?" he asked. "Do you think this ceremony can help me?"

"I know that it helped others," I said. "Our shaman, Don Rodrigo will lead you. You trust him, don't you?"

"I did feel better after I met that old guy," Ronnie said. "Yeah, that night after the tobacco treatment or ritual or whatever you want to call it, I slept like a baby, man. No flashbacks, no nightmares. That night I didn't replay an ambush in my head like I usually do. I slept sound and that hasn't happened in a long time. The old man is awesome. I do feel like I can trust him. You could tell he's done a lot of living in his time. I felt good when he called me '*mi hijo*'. Not the kind of thing my own father would usually say. When I was growing up, 'Asshole' is what he usually called me."

"Trust is important, but here's the question. Are you willing to use the discipline that you learned in the military to help yourself get better?"

"I'll try."

Ronnie reappeared at the lab the next day. "So, OK. I told Mel I'd try it. And look at this." He fished a little handheld recorder out of his pocket and flipped it on. "Testing, testing." Happy with this new gadget, he played it back for my benefit.

"Very cool." I agreed.

"You just to talk into it. You don't have to sit there and try to put words down on paper."

"Where did it come from?" I asked as though I didn't know.

"It's Mel's. He gave it to me. I'm going to record how I feel about the treatment. All you have to do is push the little button. A little green light goes on and you're ready to roll."

Mel insisted that Ronnie begin the prescribed cleansing diet right away. Even though Mel was a confirmed carnivore, he, too, was determined to 'go veg' as he called it. Gabrielle balked at cooking food she considered tasteless, but Mel had given her orders to prepare the vegetarian meals and so she followed instructions. There was to be no meat, no spicy food, and even no sweets. After meals Ronnie would return to his bunk to rest and meditate. Even though Armand, the guard supervisor grumbled, this became the ex-soldier's routine as he prepared for the ceremony ahead.

Julio and I took Ronnie to see Don Rodrigo at the herb farm. On the ride over, I noticed his hands were shaking. From where I sat in the back seat of the old white sedan, I overheard him tell Julio, "Dyin' for a joint right now."

"*Sorry, amigo,*" Julio shook his head. "No can do."

Things were quiet when we arrived. Don Rodrigo's granddaughter had gone to the village. Inside, the house felt hot and cramped. Outside, we sought the shade of a banana tree. A male quetzal bird, its plumage a vivid blue, perched overhead. Before the bird flitted off, Don Rodrigo, with a quick nod of his head, mouthed the words, "*el bendición*", acknowledging the blessing of the bird's presence.

Julio and I watched carefully as he performed the tobacco healing for Ronnie a second time. Then, the two of us went into the forest to gather the vines and the leaves for the tea.

On our return, I was surprised to see Mel sitting with Don Rodrigo and Ronnie.

How the hell did he find the place? For sure I'd never told him the way.

"People don't think of me as having a spiritual side, but I feel a real connection to this place and to the people," Mel said. "Why do you think I came to Belize in the first place?"

An unkind thought crossed my mind, but I shooed it away.

"Years ago, back when I was doing meditation with my guru, I had a vision. I was running through the jungle, barefoot, unarmed and wearing only a loin cloth. I heard footsteps from behind, like I was being chased. Over my shoulder, there was someone from another tribe running after me, waving a machete. Ahead loomed a stone temple with a chamber at the top. My only hope of escape was up the steep stairs. Inside the temple chamber I slipped behind a stone altar only to have my enemy follow me in.

Suddenly, a woman appeared in the doorway with a long spindle in her hand. Without a word, she stabbed the man who chased me. When he fell to the floor, she vanished just as quickly as she had appeared. With a jolt, I woke up, back in my body. I was myself; I was Mel Powers again. But what I has seen in the dream felt so real it made me stop and think. Could it have been past life? Pretty weird, huh?"

Ronnie listened, all ears. "Whoa, talk about a nightmare. It sounds like a scene from a movie."

Don Rodrigo spoke. "That was the goddess, Ix Chel. She protected you. And so, you should go with us to Caracol to thank her."

For Julio, too, it was time to prepare. Sharing the solemn duties of the tea ceremony with his uncle, Don Rodrigo, this would be his first time acting as a leader. Bracing himself for the challenge, Julio vowed, to forgo his usual diet of spicy food, red meat, and beer. Even more painful for him, he cancelled his usual Saturday night gig playing guitar at the bar in San Ignacio. Instead, he spent hours praying in the forest below the giant Ceiba tree, most sacred to the Maya. As Don Rodrigo saw his nephew take on a sense of connection to the healing ways of his people, he, too, became more enthusiastic.

Together Julio and his uncle checked the lunar calendar, deciding on a date for the event several days ahead. With the full moon soon approaching, conditions would be the most favorable to connect with the spirit world. Three days before, we would visit the Mayan pyramid at Caracol.

Mel wanted to be with us for the midnight walk to Caracol.

Julio and I would agree to that only if he left his guards and his guns behind.

Even though we could have driven close to the ancient site, Don Rodrigo suggested that we walk taking the path that wound through the forest from the village of San Miguel. "Julio can show you the way. You have my blessing but, sadly, I won't be able to go with you," he said. "My knees are not up to the journey."

Caracol was once the center of a mighty kingdom built by the ancient Maya. Overgrown with vegetation for centuries, it remained hidden in the dense jungle until it was rediscovered by a local man looking for mahogany to harvest. Soon an unpaved road was built to the site. Once the word spread, archaeologists descended, and excavation was underway. By day, it's become quite a tourist attraction but by night it's dark, remote and silent.

Walking the last mile to Caracol would allow us to prepare our awareness as we came closer to the main structure, the huge stone mound, rising in the forest. Julio called it the Pyramid of the Great Jaguar. A light breeze quickened in the darkness and as we walked, it felt like we were the only people in the world. Julio stopped along the way, asking for permission from the spirits. Drawing closer to the pyramid, Julio led us in prayers of thanks to the goddess, Ix Chel. He called on the spirits of the plants and of the forest, chanting the words I'd often heard in Don Rodrigo's prayers.

Always in a hurry to get to the next destination, Mel's impatience shone through until the night cry of a big cat broke the stillness. He slapped his sides as if looking for a weapon that thankfully wasn't there.

As we reached the ball court between the two pyramids, the moon illuminated us with celestial radiance. Standing transfixed and silent, my senses were elevated. Peace transcended the night like a mist, and I felt a renewed sense of kinship with nature. All around, the physical environment seemed to grow hazy. For a moment I felt my body lose connection to what we call reality until a gust of wind blew through, rustling the trees, and sending a flock of birds screeching off in protest.

It was a magical night. If we needed confirmation of that, a kinkajou crossed our path. The small gentle mammal the size of a large housecat stopped to stare at us, its golden eyes reflected in the flashlight. I was nervous when Ronnie held his hand out to pet the wild creature. But the animal wasn't afraid. The small golden-brown creature purred and wound his tail around Ronnie's arm, seemingly, in friendship. When the ex-soldier turned to all of us with a wondering smile, I saw a tear glint in his eye.

Ten

As part of Mel's commitment to the new undertaking, he called in local artisans. In an open space behind the lab, he had them build a gazebo about fifteen or sixteen feet across covered by the traditional thatched roof. The structure took shape quickly. At Julio's suggestion, netting was attached to a framework overhead. Once the project was finished and the workers left, Julio smudged the structure with bundles of dried herbs, calling on the spirits of the forest for strength and courage.

A few days before the ceremony, I borrowed Gabrielle's car and drove back to Don Rodrigo's farm. All was tranquil, and I found him napping in a hammock in the shade behind the small house he shared with his family. Content to be back in a space that I had grown to love, I was happy to let him sleep. Enjoying the familiar sights and smells of the garden, I sat quietly for several minutes until a stray goat strayed into the chicken coop. The cackling of angry hens broke the silence, and my teacher's eyelids fluttered open. He raised his head and looked around groggy-eyed. He would have turned to go back to sleep but then I sneezed.

"Carrie, my child, how long have you been sitting there?"

"Just a few minutes. You looked so peaceful; I didn't want to wake you. How are you?"

"How am I?" He shook his head. "*Dios mio! Mi familia esta loco.* They make me crazy."

"But they love you. Of that, there is no doubt."

"Perhaps, perhaps, but they make me tired. Sometimes I think I just want to sleep." A wan smile curved his lips.

I felt sorry for disturbing him. "I came to see if you want any help with preparing for the tea ceremony. Also, I must warn you that our friend Mel will be with us at the tea ceremony. And he is *loco* too."

"I know. He is *loco* and a little *pelegroso*, dangerous, also. But let's hope the tea ceremony will have a healing effect on him too."

"Yes, he's unpredictable, but I feel safe with you and Julio there to guide him. Who knows, perhaps, he'll be changed by the experience, in a good way."

"Yes, let us hope so. I invited *mi amiga,* Doña Luisa to join us. You know her. She is a midwife for the village and a healer, like me."

"Of course, she is a lovely person. I remember when you hurt your back. She brought you the leaves from the Santa Maria plant. Together we heated them in oil and placed them on your back."

"Since this is Julio's first time leading the ceremony with me, she'll also be there to help. I asked her to sing the icaros. The soothing songs that bring comfort to those who are taking the tea for the first time. That is all of you, yes?"

"Ronnie and Mel will all be doing it for the first time. I was with you once before. Do you remember?"

"Oh yes."

I could see that he didn't.

"There's one more thing, you must tell the others. You tell them what they eat is important. Even more important is what they don't eat. Tell Mel no beer, no whiskey, no spicy food. And tell Ronnie, no marijuana."

"Yes, yes, Julio warned us all days ago. He's been keeping track of what Ronnie eats," I laughed. "And what I eat also."

Days before, Julio and I had gone into the forest to gather the vines and the leaves that would be used. They were dried and ready now, the branches cut into lengths as long as my forearm. With the sharpest knife I could find, I shredded the bark from the vines before using a mallet to break down the inner fibers into a pulp. Taking a break from the physical work, I wiped sweat from my brow.

It would be my honor if you and I could prepare the tea together. That's why I came today."

"I'm glad you are here. I need you to help me gather one more thing from the forest. Follow me."

"What's missing?" I asked.

"The bark of the avahuma tree," he said. "It protects all of us from the spirits that cause fear, most important for Ronnie. Now bring that sharp knife and come." Grabbing his walking stick, he beckoned. "I will show you where to look."

Our walk down that path brought back memories. Countless days we had set off at dawn into the forest. On those days, I'd been forced to run after him to keep up. Now I held myself back, matching his slower gait as we walked down the path into the trees, stopping at the edge of the jungle.

"There, right there," he pointed. "Those trees. Do you see them?" There was a group of three saplings with reddish leaves next to a wild cocoa bush.

First asking the plant's permission, I cut several strips of bark from the largest sapling. I carried shavings and strips of bark to where Don Rodrigo now sat, eyes closed, in the shade of a coconut palm.

Back at the house, there was the hard work of grinding the vines, the leaves and bark shavings together. As I sweated over it, my teacher muttered prayers for the safety of all who would partake of the ceremony. Work done, we walked out into the late afternoon sunshine.

"I should go," I said. "I should get Gabrielle's car back."

"Not yet. Come quick, while it's quiet, before they come back," he said. He beckoned conspiratorially. "I want you to do something for me, something very important."

Inside, I followed him to the back of the house. Grabbing my hand for support, he slowly lowered himself to the floor next to the metal bedframe where he'd slept for so many years. From beneath it he brought out a woven bag. "Here, take this."

For a brief second, he opened it wide enough for me to see. Inside there were dozens of neatly folded bills of every denomination, rubber-banded together. "Take this to the lodge and give the money to James. Ask him to keep it safe for me."

As he pushed the bag into my hands, I realized this must be his life savings. It was the accumulation of small bills accepted from the hands of humble patients he'd cared for over the decades. His life's work. The look on his face prevented any questions.

All I could do was to stammer, "Of course I will."

"I trust James. I want him to keep it for me. If anything happens, tell him it belongs to Julio. I don't want any of the rest of them to find it." He stretched out his hand, and I tugged him up from the floor.

"Wait, I know you trust James, but don't you at least want me to count it?"

"*Si, si, si.* You can if you want. But I know how much is in there. Now take it."

End of discussion.

Outside, he watched me lock the bag in the Gabrielle's trunk. Just then the peaceful afternoon was shattered by the rumblings of a car engine sputtering into the farmyard.

My teacher clapped his hand to his forehead. "*Mala suerte,* bad luck. They're back," he groaned. "Here, I want to give you something else." From his pocket, he slipped an object, no bigger than a small pebble into my hand. "Take this, quick." Before I could look at it, he closed my fingers around the object. "Put it away. Don't lose it."

It felt smooth and cool.

Before I could say more, Josefina, drove up, barely missing the bumper of Gabrielle's car. She parked the family's ancient sedan and turned off the engine. She got out with two small children trailing behind her. "*Papi,* whose car is that?" Her eyes narrowed, as she looked in my direction. "Oh, it's you."

"Hello, Josefina," I said. "How are you?"

Don Rodrigo waved his hand as if he were shooing me away. "You must go now. Take it and go quickly," he said.

Before I drove away, I looked at what he had given me. It was a beautiful green jade carving of a toad.

As the jungle's shadows deepened, heat lightning flickered across the sky. The only participants at the tea ceremony would be Ronnie, Mel and me. Not a large gathering. Julio suggested we add one more participant. Perhaps, Gabrielle, Mel's girlfriend?

Mel shook his head. "Just the three of us will be fine," he said

Once the sun had set, we gathered in the gazebo. Julio placed us in a circle around the shelter. We were ready, and a ball of excitement filled my core. I was happy to see Doña Luisa, the short, brown-skinned woman standing quietly next to my teacher. Her dark eyes looked out kindly from a face weathered by years of living.

As the moon rose, we watched Don Rodrigo roll the dry leaves of tobacco into a sphere. Before placing them in a pipe made from the root of the Ceiba tree, he sprinkled crushed herbs on top. When all was ready, be brought flame to the pipe bowl. The tobacco ritual was the first step in a cleansing that would continue through the night. As Don Rodrigo stood before Mel, a smell of tobacco mixed with the aromatic herbs hovered above us, drifting into the night air. Mel squirmed in his seat like a kid. Unfazed, Don Rodrigo brushed Mel's eyes closed before exhaling the pungent mixture over his head, and shoulders. He went to Ronnie next, and as the billows of smoke wafted above him, the ex-soldier relaxed with a sigh. I was next. Breathing in deeply, the tobacco tickled my nose.

Don Rodrigo and Julio stepped outside to the open fire where the tea, made from plant essence, bubbled. The two men took turns stirring the vat of liquid. When it was ready, Don Rodrigo scooped out a dipper-full of the brew. Pouring the liquid from the dipper into a mug, he transferred the steaming brew from mug to dipper and back again, waiting for the beverage to cool. When all was ready, he divided the tea into small cups, one for each of us to drink.

Mel went first, gulping until the cup was empty. "*Lentamente,* go slow, go slow," Don Rodrigo said. "Not so much."

Ronnie did the same. When it was my turn, I sipped at the bitter mixture. Don Rodrigo stood beside me, waiting until I drained all the liquid in the cup.

In the dim candlelight, Julio took the center of the space and began a chant. Our eyes were alert and questioning, waiting for what would come next. As I listened, the words seemed to come from a distance, growing fainter and fainter. After some minutes, Ronnie sat up, a startled look on his face. Suddenly, he ran out into the night. On his return a few minutes later, his expression was difficult to read.

It was Mel's turn next. He bolted, running out into the darkness. We heard sounds of gagging in the warm jungle air. I was not surprised when my stomach began to churn, and soon I was lurching out into the night. Supporting myself against a tree, an internal spasm sent the contents of my stomach pitching onto the ground. More internal tremors followed. Once my stomach was empty, I allowed myself a few moments rest before I staggered back into the communal space. Once the purge was over, it was time to rest. Each of us had prepared pallets to make ourselves comfortable. Now we sought refuge in the cushions waiting for us.

As Julio turned in a circle, he called on each of the nine benevolent spirits by name. When the wind picked up it was as though they were heeding the call. Doña Luisa began her song, repeating the phrases over and over, the sounds sweet and soothing, like a lullaby. Though the words were unknown to me, I seemed to grasp their meaning.

The night sounds of the jungle grew faint as Julio lowered the netting. We closed our eyes. The inward journey had begun. Like a leaf fluttering slowly to the ground, I drifted into a trance. My thoughts turned to Don Rodrigo and his gift. I reached for it in my pocket. As I held it in my hand, the small stone fetish grew warm, seeming to vibrate. I heard a buzzing, as though a rattle was being shaken somewhere close by. As I shook my head to clear the sound, I fell into a space between sleep and wakefulness.

Strangely, I felt neither fear nor surprise as I saw myself at the edge of a lake, climbing on the back of a giant green toad. As the toad broke the water's surface, we plunged together, through murky water, touching bottom. At that point, a reed drifted past. I grasped it and held it to my chest. Slowly the toad turned, swimming upward, breaking the surface of the water, then gliding to shore. I stepped onto dry land, but before the creature returned to its watery home, I felt a sense of trust pass between us. There were no words. The time passed slowly by.

It seemed hours, minutes, years were all one. I woke at dawn, stiff, cold and exhausted. Lifting my head from the pillow I sought out my fellow participants. Mel was still asleep while Ronnie sat silently, tears streaming down his face. Don Rodrigo slept soundly. Next to him, Doña Luisa rested her head on his shoulder. I heard running water and saw Julio in the outdoor shower, his face turned upward to the water. When he felt me watching, he shook the water from his hair, letting his dark eyes rest on my face as he smiled. My face grew warm and the tug at my heart surprised me.

Eleven

The yellow light filtered through the palm fronds overhead. Two macaws, their red feathers like flashes of fire, flitted from tree to tree. After hours spent in utter darkness, my senses felt heightened as morning flooded into the gazebo.

There was movement nearby. Footsteps scuffing up the wooden steps jostled my hearing. A soft voice asked, "*Señor* are you thirsty?"

Don Rodrigo stirred, opening his eyes He looked up at Gabrielle and nodded eagerly. From a tall glass pitcher, she poured out a tumbler of water laced with sliced lemon. He drained the glass in two gulps, asking, "*Mas agua, por favor.*" He drank the second glass eagerly. With a flirtatious wink and a smile, he patted her hand and whispered something I couldn't hear. She held a finger to her lips, looking over at Mel, still asleep, in a sign not to wake him. The old man laughed as he watched her wander back to the house.

Across the yard, Julio emerged bare-chested from the outdoor shower. From where I sat, I could see the water glistening on his back and shoulders. I should have averted my gaze, given him a few more well-deserved moments of privacy but somehow, I was riveted. It was as if he had grown overnight. Today he stood tall, radiating a new air of maturity, an aura of calm. It felt was as though his broad shoulders had carried us through the night and I was grateful.

Off to my right Ronnie yawned hugely, sat up and stretched, arms reaching high overhead. "I feel like a kid again," he said, as though speaking to the air. "Is that possible?"

Surprised by the warmth I felt toward him, I reached over to place my hand on his. "The world can sometimes be a beautiful place."

"I feel like I been reborn," he said, a look of wonder crossing his features. "When I got out of the service, back from Iraq, I wondered the hell just happened?"

Sympathy filled my heart. "Tell me more."

"Whenever I closed my eyes, trying to sleep, all I could see was the faces of the Iraqi people, all the death we'd caused. I was always feeling ashamed, but this morning, I feel different." He wiped his eyes.

"Did you ever think that you might have been a victim, too?" I asked.

He nodded. "I didn't want anybody to go through what I been through. All the rage I felt, all those meds they gave me at the VA hospital. It drove me nuts."

Minutes later, Mel stirred. He stood up, looking over at where we sat. "Hey, dude. How are you feeling?" At the sight of Ronnie's tears, he moved closer, putting an arm around the younger man's shoulders.

"I didn't know what to expect," Ronnie said in a voice filled with surprise.

"Let's walk." Mel led Ronnie away from the gazebo toward the house.

As they moved away, I heard Ronnie. "That was deep. I almost feel like I can forgive myself for what happened."

"It hit me too, man." Mel said. "Really kicked my ass."

"What should I do now?" Ronnie asked.

"You don't have to do anything now. Take the rest of the day off." Mel sounded kind, almost fatherly. "Then I want you to take out that little gizmo I gave you, the little recorder? When you're ready, find a quiet spot and record everything you remember. How you felt last night. Can you do that?"

Ronnie agreed and I decided to give myself the day off too. I needed rest. I was wondering if Julio might feel the same way, but he was helping his uncle into the old white Ford. I waved and called to them to wait. Then I remembered. The money! It was still in the trunk of Gabrielle's car. "I'll just be a minute." I ran toward the main house.

I found Gabrielle in the kitchen. When I asked her for the car keys, she tossed them to me. I ran out, opened the trunk, my heart in my mouth. With happy relief I saw the bag where I'd left it, stuffed under a spare tire in the corner. I shoved it into my backpack, returned the keys and ducked, shame-faced, into the back seat of Julio's car. We sped off down the road. Julio dropped me off at the lodge. Then he and his uncle returned to the relative quiet of the herb farm.

I awoke hours later as a rosy twilight seeped through the windows of my now familiar room. After spending almost twelve hours sleeping off the effects of the previous night, I stretched, luxuriating in the soft pillows and crisp sheets. Feeling like a privileged character, I curled into a ball on the bed. My thoughts turned to Don Rodrigo and his gift resting where I'd left it on the night table next to the bed. Holding it in my hand, the small stone fetish seemed to grow warm and pulsate.

I drifted off and when I woke again it was the morning of the next day. Had I really slept around the clock, not once but twice? Outside birds chirped, water lapped against the rocks of the lagoon, and guests murmured to each other as they walked the garden paths.

I took a long shower, soaking my head under the stream of water for a long time, trying to untangle where the previous twenty-four hours had gone. With one thing left undone, I dressed, grabbed my backpack and walked toward the main lodge building. Inside, I took in the empty tables in the dining room. I guessed that most of the lodge guests had already breakfasted and were on their way to spots of local interest. No doubt the kitchen staff, after the morning rush, was ready to take a mid-morning break.

From her usual spot at the front desk, Gloria smiled a welcome. "How are you?" she asked kindly. "Haven't seen much of you lately."

"A little tired. Just working hard." The backpack of Don Rodrigo's life savings felt heavy on my arm. "Is James here?"

"No, he's at a meeting about poachers. Rangers found two dead jaguars, their paws missing. Killed by thieves. It's horrible, just horrible."

I winced at the image of the beautiful jungle cats, now on an endangered species list, being killed for body parts to be sold on the international market. "I've heard of things like that happening in Africa, with the rhino horns, but I didn't think anything like that would happen here."

"Not so different, I'm afraid. Just like there, Central America is a region with so much poverty, it causes people to do terrible things," she said.

"I wonder if I could ask a favor," I said, holding up the full backpack. "Would you put this in the safe for me? It belongs to Don Rodrigo."

She motioned me to follow her and we headed to the office. I watched as she hovered over the large safe behind the desk. Dialing in the safe's combination, the tumblers clicked into place and the door swung open. As Gloria stuffed the parcel inside, I breathed a sigh of relief. The money was safe and that was enough for now. Maybe I'd wait until James returned and together, he and I would discuss how to make the old healer's life savings more secure. Snapping the safe closed, Gloria headed back out to the floor.

"Gloria, just one more thing." I followed in her wake.

"Sure."

"I'd love to show you something."

At the sight of the small green jade amulet, her eyes shone. "Oooh! I want to touch but I know it's only for you."

I turned to the window, letting the light shine through.

"I've never seen one like this before. Where did you find it?"

"It was a gift from Don Rodrigo, but I felt foolish asking him about it. I was hoping that you or James might have seen something like this before in your travels?"

"I can't help you but there is someone who might know. Come, let's go find Maria. She must be in the kitchen."

As we walked my stomach growled, reminding me that it was well over twenty-four hours since my last meal.

Before she could say more, one of the staff called out, "Gloria, the tour bus is here."

With a shrug she turned to me as if to say, 'What can I do?'

"Gloria, no problem. I'll find Maria. I know what she looks like."

As though conjured up, the handsome, solid-looking Maya woman pushed her hip through the kitchen's swinging door. Balancing a platter of eggs and tortillas in one hand and her coffee pot in the other, she navigated her way into the lodge dining room placing the food on the buffet nearby. It smelled delicious.

When I called her name, Maria turned, her broad face cocked to the side in surprise. A smile quickly replaced the quizzical look and she held out her coffee pot. "*Café, Señorita?*"

"Oh, not right now, thanks. But those eggs look delicious."

She looked to the buffet. "Shall I get you some?"

"No thank you, I'll help myself in a minute but first I wondered if I could show you something. Gloria said you might know what this means." I unzipped the pouch and let the toad icon fall into my palm. Again, it felt warm and vibrant.

Maria's eyes shone as she peeked into my hand. "*Dios mio, Señorita.* Where did you find this?" she asked.

"It was a gift, a gift from Don Rodrigo. It almost feels alive."

She smiled then and nodded her agreement. "Rodrigo? *Si, si, si.* I am proud to say that he is my cousin." With those words, Maria, barely five feet tall seemed to grow taller. "I know him very well. He helps my family and all of the people in our village of San Mateo."

"I know, he's important to me and all of us who live here. I was hoping you might be able to tell me the meaning of this icon."

She looked at it closely. "Yes. The toad is a sign of change. As a toad moves between air and water, it can breathe in two different worlds. The person who follows the sign of this animal must learn to live in two different worlds. Often, they experience a change in the heart to make this happen."

With those words, Maria's eyes became serious and the smile faded from her lips. "The person who holds this will find the rewards are great, but the challenges are even more difficult. Not many people can be ready for this but if Don Rodrigo gave this to you, well, he must believe you are ..." Her voice trailed off.

I am what?

As though reading my thoughts, she replied. "You should go ask him. He will tell you."

I had been visited by the spirit of the toad, but was I changed? I had put the vision out of my thoughts. It was too surreal, but as she spoke those words, it had all come back to me with a sense of truth that I couldn't deny.

"Thank you, Maria. I need to tell him about the dream I had." She smiled and covered my hand with her own. I felt a great energy pass between us.

Twelve

Deep in thought, I wandered along a hibiscus scented path on my way to the lodge dining room. After my recent tea ceremony experience, I wanted to share my encounter with someone but was there anyone nearby who would understand what I had lived through? Sadly, the answer to that question was, "no". Before I could dwell further on my unwelcome sense of solitude, youthful laughter broke the silence. A voice called, "Carrie, Carrie. Wait up."

I looked around, surprised, then overjoyed to see my student pals waving to me. "Wow, you three are a welcome sight," I said. "I thought you might be gone for good. I really missed you guys. Where were you?"

Fair-haired Ellen wore a newly acquired sunburn. She gave me a big hug. "Just got back from a week in Guatemala and we had such an amazing time. Are you going to dinner?"

"Yes. C'mon, the wine is on me."

Overflowing with details of their latest trek to the magnificent Mayan ruin at Tikal in Guatemala, my new friends were excited about an annual ceremony that took place on the main plaza in front of the Mayan temple. As we ate and talked, they passed around their phones, showing photos and videos of a large gathering of Guatemalan families in colorful hand-woven clothing. A video taken by Josh showed family groups as they circled the altar in front of the main temple. A bonfire sent points of flame shooting into the dusky evening sky. Participants, young and old, each held a burning candle. Chanting ancient prayers, they all knelt on the hard stones.

Overwhelmed by the experience, my friends shared feelings of awe. Margo was thoughtful as she talked about how moved she was as they watched. "We're Americans, so for us, things are always supposed to be the newest and the latest. I can't imagine how it must feel to be part of such an ancient culture."

Josh agreed, "They were paying homage, not only to their ancestors but to the structures built so many years in the past. And to the spirits that still dwell there. You could almost feel them."

Dinner was over and we'd already killed two bottles of wine. Waiting for dessert to arrive, I finally felt ready to reveal my recent adventure. Producing the jade amulet from my pocket, I shared my own sense of excitement as my three friends peered at the small figure. Each of them came up with a theory on the symbolism of the jade talisman. I hadn't talked to anyone about my recent experiences, but after I described my vision, I soon found myself sharing all I could remember of the tea ceremony. Don Rodrigo's mixing the beverage, Julio's chants and Donã Luisa's songs calling on the spirits of the forest. Then there was the drinking of the tea, the purge, the waves of energy and the personal imagery of my own spiritual journey, traveling to the underworld on the back of the toad. Finally, there was a sense of release along with the separation of mind and body that came afterwards.

Though the three friends met while attending graduate school in New Mexico, they all grew up in California, a place they laughingly referred to as, 'The land of what's happening now.' They claimed that everything trendy took place in their home state. When I first broached the subject of the tea ceremony and my part in it, Josh said, "Oh yeah, you mean ayahuasca? Tea ceremonies are the big thing now in California, especially in San Francisco. I guess that's no surprise, is it?"

"Josh, you tried it, didn't you?" Margo asked.

"Yeah, you have to be careful. Last summer I was visiting my buddy at Berkeley. We decided to participate in a tea ceremony with a group of other students. But what my friend didn't tell the ceremony leader that he was taking anti-depressants. I had a pretty positive experience, but my poor friend became disoriented during the ceremony. It was a bad trip for the poor guy. He was hallucinating, scratching himself for hours, saying his skin was crawling."

I wondered how different the experience might feel if it were conducted in a bricks and mortar setting. I felt thankful to have been outside surrounded by the forest.

As if Josh read my thoughts, he said, "For sure, it would have been much better to be outdoors in the warm air, nature all around. We were cooped up in a chilly, empty hall."

"Before the ceremony, I was concerned about Ronnie. He suffers from PTSD. And really, Ronnie was the reason for the event in the first place," I said. "Even so, I wasn't sure how it would turn out."

"So, how was it for him?' Josh asked.

"It changed his entire outlook. He told me he felt like he was reborn. The experience was a very positive…" I stopped in mid-sentence. Before I could give more thought to Ronnie and how he was feeling, I was surprised to see Mel walk in.

He scanned the room, but his gaze missed the corner where we sat. His focus was drawn across the room to a table for two by the veranda, the only other seat occupied by a bold looking blond with a sleek hairdo and a manner to match.

From where I sat in a corner of the crowded dining room, I doubted he'd seen me. He looked preoccupied, making straight for the striking woman who beckoned to him from across the room. She pointed to herself as if to indicate that she might be who he was looking for.

Could this be Mel's new romance?

Maybe not. As he said his name, seeming to introduce himself, heads turned in their direction. She replied, "Roz Becker." As they shook hands I heard, "It's great to finally meet the legendary Mel Powers."

Mel usually can't keep his voice down, especially when talking about himself, but not this time. Straining my ears, it was no use. I couldn't hear a word.

"Ellen," I said, "don't turn around. Over by the veranda, that's Mel, the guy I'm working with."

Making a big show of dropping her napkin, Ellen took a good look over her shoulder as she picked it up. "The guy sitting with the blond," she said.

I nodded. "Do me a favor, take a walk to the restroom and see if you can hear what they're talking about. It's your chance to play secret agent so, don't be obvious."

"I'm on it," she said.

Getting up from the table, she put a finger to her lips. Margo and Josh cracked up as Ellen mugged. Luckily, Mel was so engrossed in conversation that their laughter went unnoticed in the crowded dining room.

Mel motioned to a waiter for a cup of coffee. Once he downed the brew, he stood, ushering the woman out of the dining room. With Mel in his usual bush jacket and rough boots and his new friend in tailored black and heels, they made for a mismatched pair.

As I watched them go, Ellen turned around and made a beeline back to our table. "What were they talking about?" I asked.

"Well, it wasn't a date if that's what you were wondering. I could hear them say a few words like, pharmaceuticals, IPO, the FDA. Then I think they noticed me looking at them and after that, they lowered their voices. I couldn't hear any more."

Now it was my turn to play spy. Almost without thinking, I stood, announcing I'd be right back but instead of heading to the restroom, I followed Mel and the woman out of the dining room. Stealthily tracking them as they walked down the path toward one of the largest cabanas, I hung back, hiding behind a tree as the blond woman unlocked the cabana door. She and Mel went inside.

I returned quickly to my friends at the table. "I can't stay. I'm sorry."

"But we didn't have dessert yet," Margo reminded me.

"I'll explain later," I dropped some bills on the table to cover my share of the food and the two bottles of wine I'd ordered. Out into the jungle darkness, the toad amulet felt warm in my pocket. Was it urging me on?

Yes.

Hadn't I been told that the toad was a symbol of wisdom and self-reliance? Now it was time for me to live up to the gift that my teacher had given me. And I was determined to know what they were talking about. On instinct I moved off the path and crept around the outside corner of the large cabana Mel and his new friend had entered. By its size alone, I could see that it was a departure from the lodge's more modest one-room accommodations. I remembered hearing the staff refer to it as "the villa" because it had its own kitchen and sitting room.

It was a breezy night, and fragrant stirrings filled the darkness, but the light wind did little to cool the heat surging through me. Perching on tiptoe, I peered over the windowsill, anxious to get a look inside. There was Mel was seated on a stool near the glossy, well-appointed kitchen. As he craned his neck, peering around, I imagined him making a quick estimate of the cost of the accommodation.

Focusing my hearing on the inside of the suite, I blessed the Belize style architecture. Interior cooling was provided by a fan silently circling at the top of the pitched ceiling. A tropical fondness for wide open windows, free of glass allowed me to hear the conversation clearly.

Across from Mel, his new friend settled herself on the sofa. She seemed to be doing most of the talking. "You may be wondering why I got in touch with you," she said. "We actually have an attorney in common, Jason Winkler."

Mel nodded, "Yes, Jason. It's been a while."

"When I mentioned the trip I planned to Belize, he told me you were here and suggested I might look you up. Without breaking client privilege, of course, he mentioned that you'd been able to put something together with the Belize government."

"Yes, of course. I've been working on a few projects around creating jobs. For now, things are just in the development stage," Mel said.

Oh, he's playing it close to the vest.

"Well, your reputation speaks volumes and I know that as a tech entrepreneur you were very successful."

"Yes, but those were different times."

"Yes, different, but still, very good times for you," Roz said.

Mel smiled but said nothing.

"Things change but one thing remains constant. You seem to

have a way of being, shall I say, proactive. That, and your timing is good," Roz continued. "I'm sure you're aware that many pharmaceutical products on the market are plant derived."

"Of course."

"Belize has opened up to the outside world, still, many people would have trouble finding it on a map. Yet, its tropical forest plants have been a source of medicine for hundreds of years."

"Yes, I've heard that," Mel murmured.

"That's why I'm here and perhaps you are too." Roz straightened her posture. "I wonder if you have heard of our latest venture, Eureka Pharmaceuticals."

Mel shook his head, no, but I was sure he was paying attention.

"Eureka is focused on the sources of the plant-based wisdom. Our goal is to connect with the traditional healers of the region to learn of their secrets. It's the concept of bioprospecting. Interested?"

"I've been working with some of the same ideas," Mel said. "I've connected with the government in hopes we can be of service to the indigenous people of this country." Mel seemed to search for his words. "We've heard of some of the successes of indigenous healers, but I have yet to actually make much contact."

That's a relief. For once I'm glad Mel decided to lie.

In the trees overhead, a bird screeched at my presence. It gave me a scare and I slipped from my perch, falling with a thud, into the bushes.

Roz stood and moved to the veranda. "What was that?" she asked, looking out into the dark.

"Probably just a damn howler monkey," Mel said. "They think they own the place."

I crouched on the ground outside, praying. *Don't let them see me.*

"Where was I?" Roz said.

"Eureka," Mel supplied.

I held my breath, waiting for the right moment. Clouds drifted across the moon providing a cover of darkness. My fingers sought the ledge and I hoisted myself back into position.

"Yes, we're a San Francisco-based company focused on isolating bioactive compounds. We're looking for tropical plants with a history of medicinal use," Roz said.

"Interesting concept," Mel said.

"And who would know that better than the local healers and shaman? And Belize has many. Eureka, as I mentioned, is founded on the concept of bioprospecting. And our goal is to share the benefits of the shamanic wisdom with the modern world. At the same time, we also hope to give back to the indigenous people."

"My group is also exploring traditional medicines that have a direct therapeutic healing approach," Mel said.

Is he talking about our aborted mission to find an antibiotic? The one never got off the ground?

"Of course, Eureka's second goal is to promote the conservation of tropical forests and to bridge the gap between the needs of indigenous cultures and the rest of the global population."

"Well, it sounds like we're in agreement on that. How can we help each other?" Roz said. "You've been here longer that I have. My associate will be joining me in a day or two. He's an ethnobotanist with extensive experience in Central America. He'll be leading the field research team."

Oh, my God. Ethnobotanist? There aren't all that many of us. Who could it be?

"For now, I'm wondering if you might help me contact someone. His name is Don Rodrigo. I've heard he's a well-respected healer and he lives nearby. Have you met him?"

My throat tightened and I held my breath waiting for Mel's response.

"Rodrigo? Of course, he's a legend. Now that you mention it, we've been talking about working together on a project."

"What's so fascinating to us is that a traditional healer, like your friend, Don Rodrigo has spent decades at his work. As he treats his patients, one on one, you could almost say that he's been conducting his own experiments with the plants. Over the years, he's come to know what works and what doesn't work. It's almost like he's created his own set of clinical trials." She laughed at her own wit.

"That's an interesting take, I must say."

"You must tell me more about this Don Rodrigo. I'd love to come and visit your compound. When I visited the Belize Economic Development Minister, he told me you have a lab on site. True?"

"I've been doing some work there, but I'm afraid what we're working on is proprietary."

"I see," Roz said. "Any interest in investors, or partners? Or are you just in it for the cause?"

Sphinx-like, Mel's expression was not easy to read. "Still open to ideas. Let's just call it a work in progress."

"As I mentioned, my business associate is flying in tomorrow. He's worked with other indigenous healers. I'd love for him to hear more about what you've been working on. Any chance we could set up a meeting at your compound?"

"I can't make any promises but let me check my schedule," Mel said.

A picture bloomed in my mind. I saw one of my books of notes, thoughtlessly left sitting on the counter in the laboratory. I had to secure it, without delay. The only thing that mattered now was my research and I didn't want anyone like Roz to even know it existed.

Thirteen

Moving backward, my feet found solid ground and I crouched away from the window as silently as I could. Back on the gravel path, I stopped briefly to straighten my spine. It felt so good that I cricked my neck back forth before I slipped away through the trees. I chose a roundabout route back to the lodge to avoid Mel in case he were to emerge unexpectedly from the meeting. Still, why should I hide? I'd done nothing wrong. Truth be told, for once, maybe the same could be said of Mel.

Was it too late to call Julio? Maybe, but I dialed anyway, and he picked up. "What's up? Carrie? Everything OK?"

"Can you do me a favor, Julio? I need to get something from the lab." There was music and laughter in the background.

Damn, It's Saturday night. His weekend gig playing guitar.

A female voice called his name, giggles followed.

"I'm at the club right now but, I can take you tomorrow. Will that work?"

"No worries, I'll figure something out. Have fun."

Was there somebody else I could cadge a ride from, maybe somebody on the hotel staff? Maria perhaps, or even James?

The white lodge van was missing from its usual spot off to

the right of the lodge dining room. But there was Mel's SUV parked under a palm tree. Cautiously, I sidled up to it, wanting to make sure there were no surprises inside.

Empty, thank God.

Then I tried the rear door. Amazed to find it unlocked, I crept in and went prone on the floor. Minutes passed.

Why did I drink all that wine? Now I gotta pee. Do I dare?

No one around. The coast was clear, so I cracked the door, ran to the bushes and got back to the SUV just in time. Footsteps on gravel came closer, keys jingled, and the interior light blazed. I held my breath and pushed my spine closer to the floor.

Mel slid in behind the wheel, then got out again. "Hey, James," he called out. "Great to see you."

"Here for dinner?" James asked.

"Business appointment with one of the guests."

"Yes, I think I can guess. Productive meeting?"

"Maybe, we'll see. Wanted to ask you something. Do you know who owns that property that abuts mine off the Georgetown Road? The one near my place, where they were building?"

"Developer from Texas. Jerry Macklin's his name. In over his head from the look of things. Two samples built, but no takers. Interested?"

"Maybe. Just thinking about something."

"I have the guy's card inside if you want it. I think he's back in the States now." "OK, let me grab it while I'm here."

A few minutes later, Mel got back in the car and we drove off into the night. At the compound, the gates clanged open and Mel pulled into his usual spot. I waited for him to go inside. A door banged shut and a few minutes later the lights went out. The sounds of the jungle night filled the air.

As I cracked the car door, the interior light sliced the dark.

Please let the dogs be tied up.

Slipping out, I made it to the lab door without mishap, dug out the key and found the lock. Inside, there on the counter was my notebook open, face down where I'd left it. Seconds later, a beam of light blazed through the window. The lab door opened. A flashlight hit me full in the face, and I held up an arm to shield my eyes.

"Oh, Carrie, it's you."

Thank God, Ronnie.

"What are you doing here?

"I forgot something."

"But why the down low? You might have gotten hurt." He looked outside. "How'd you get here? Where's your car?"

"Hitched a ride. Didn't want to make a fuss. Didn't see anybody so, I just snuck over the fence. But you're right. I should've come through the gate. Anyway, I'm glad to see you. How are you doing after the other night?" It was the first time we really had a chance to talk.

"Good. In fact, better than good. It feels like I did five years of therapy in one night. When it first starts, it's like the tea ceremony shows you your old life. Right off, I had a vision. It was like I was on the streets of Fallujah. The smells, the heat, the dust, all of it came back to me.

I started to panic when suddenly, an eagle swept down. When it covered me with its wings, and I felt a sense of protection. The cloud of fear lifted. It went dark and the next thing I knew, the eagle was leading me through a cave until we came out into the light. When I woke up, I felt like a new person. Maybe after a few more sessions, I'll control my fear instead of letting it control me. Does that make sense?"

"Yes, it does. I had quite an experience myself. Some of my own fears came up and I looked at them. Now I find myself doing things I might not have done before the ceremony." I touched the jade icon in my pocket.

"I hear you." Ronnie gave me a fist bump.

"Now, I'm here. I guess I have to stay until morning. Can you bring me a blanket or something? This concrete floor is hard."

I woke stiff and sweaty, red ants crawling up my arm. Not the best night ever. Ronnie's blanket was stiff and itchy. Didn't smell too good either but, he'd tried. I gave Julio some time and then called him to come rescue me.

It was Sunday morning, but the dogs didn't know that. When Julio's car pulled in, they put up a ruckus that brought an unhappy Mel outside in his underwear. "What the fuck! What's going on?"

I shoved the book in Julio's hands. "Put this in the car." I approached a frowning Mel on the veranda. "Morning Mel, hope I didn't wake you."

"Whaddya doing here, Carrie?"

"I needed to get something from the lab." I wondered if he might decide to tell me of his latest venture.

"In fact, I'm glad you're here." His frown faded. "There's something I want to run by you. Come inside for a minute."

Might be nice if you put your pants on.

Inside, Gabrielle puttered around, making coffee. She beckoned from the kitchen, holding up a cup in a silent offer.

Mel motioned me over to a table and found pencil and paper. "This just came to me. Thinking about expanding the compound, adding some property." He sketched the road, the gate, his house, the lab and the newly built pavilion where we'd performed the ceremony. Then a fence. On the other side of the fence were two squares that I took to be houses. He tapped them with his pencil. "What do you think?"

"Looks good."

"Since we built the pavilion, we need more space. If we want to grow this treatment idea with Don Rodrigo, we need room."

"Sure." I wondered where this was heading. Did it have anything to do with Roz?

"Anyhow there's that new development down the road."

"Yes, I noticed they put up a gate."

"They have a couple of sample houses built but I heard they're having money trouble. It might be a good time to make an offer on what they've done so far. Stop somebody else from grabbing it. Then expand our operation." He drew a road connecting the two pieces of ground.

"Expand it to what?"

"Clinical trials." He looked pleased with himself.

"Clinical trials for what?"

"We could try to get the ayahuasca into pill form. You can see how it helped our friend, Ronnie. What do you think?"

The questions were piling up.

Who would be the subjects of these trials, where would they peformed and by whom?

"Carrie, I want you to hook me up with Don Rodrigo. Get him to show me how he makes the ayahuasca."

Are you kidding?

"Talk to Don Rodrigo? Sure, he'll talk to you, but I don't expect that he's going to share the wisdom and knowledge of his people, accumulated over the years. I first met him almost three years ago and it took months before he would trust me enough to let me observe him while he worked with his patients. And that was before he had to slow down, and his family came to live with him."

"I think you're wrong there. He and I can talk man-to-man. You'll see."

Outside, beyond earshot, Julio stood talking to Ronnie. If he'd heard what Mel just said he would have laughed in his face.

Mel looked over my shoulder. "Oh, right. There's what's his name." He pointed. "Your assistant, Juan, no Julio, right? Maybe he might be open to helping me make a deal with the old man. What do you think?"

Our conversation was cut short by the sounds of a helicopter hovering over the compound. Mel looked up, checked his watch. Then his phone rang. As Mel took the call, he gestured to Ronnie to come over. "I'm gonna turn you over to my ex-Navy Seal, Ronnie." he said to whoever was on the other end.

Ex-Navy Seal?

"OK, OK, here's Ronnie. He'll bring you in to land." He handed off the phone. "Ronnie, take this while I get dressed. You know what to do. Tell him where to land. Let him put it down on the road out front. Just make sure there's no traffic."

Phone in hand, Ronnie snapped to attention, standing up straighter. As he walked through the gate, out to the road, Julio and I tagged along at a safe distance, interested to see what would happen. Even we could see the road wouldn't be wide enough. Ronnie took in the situation, moving beyond the compound. We watched his maneuvers as he guided the chopper away from the trees and brush toward an open field running along the other side of the dirt road.

As the whirring blades of the two-person chopper bent the tall meadow grasses, the craft dropped, landing safely. The pilot leaned out from the cockpit, giving Ronnie a thumbs up. "Dude, thanks," he called.

Minutes later, Mel, in bush gear, emerged from the house. Ducking across the field, he climbed in. Wordlessly, he gave the pilot the high sign and the two-person chopper lifted with the usual amount of updraft and noise. Ronnie waved them off.

Julio called out, "Good job, man."

And I felt like applauding too. Now with Mel gone, Julio and I were free to go. We jumped into his car, ready to hit the gas when Ronnie stopped us at the gate.

"Mel's outta here. Won't be back any time soon. How about I go with you to see the Old Man?" He looked at Julio.

"Sure, hop in."

"Cover for me." Ronnie called out to the other guard on duty.

As the gate clanged shut, I asked Julio to make a quick turn into the adjacent property, the one Mel proposed as a possible addition to his compound. I was curious to see more of what it looked like and how it might fit in with Mel's newest version of what he now called "our operation."

A roadside sign announced, "Palomar Estates, a Gated Resort Community." Down the gravel drive were two small bungalows, pretty typical Belize tourist housing. The one-story frame structures looked to be maybe 20 feet by 30 feet each, painted pastel yellow with turquoise shutters.

It was Sunday so there was no sign of workmen or building materials. Julio parked, but he and Ronnie stayed put as I got out to explore. The wooden porch made peeking through the front windows easy. It was a work in progress with raw wood flooring, bare walls, no furniture, and no appliances in what could have been the kitchen. Near the front door, a single brochure sat yellowing in the tropical sun. Full color illustrations featured a fantasy version of Palomar Estates with a swimming pool, palm trees and flowers.

I folded the brochure, tucking it into a pocket for future reference. Who knew what tomorrow might bring? Mel's enthusiasms were often short lived and likely to shift. Like the fading brochure, today's version of reality might include a real estate acquisition next to his property but even that might change by tomorrow.

Behind the sample houses, a path led down to the river. Around a bend, the rippling current drew my eye toward the small eddy fed by a spring spouting from a rock formation above. It formed a lovely little waterfall surrounded by leaves. With the blue sky and fleecy clouds overhead reflected in the water, I imagined how calming it might feel it float in the pool.

My revery was broken by the sound of a car horn. "Carrie, let's go."

I ran to where Julio revved the engine, anxious to take off. I scrambled back to the car. The two dropped me at the lodge. Ronnie gave a friendly wave from the passenger seat as he and Julio took off.

Back in my room, I hugged the notebook to my chest. Happy to have it back in my possession, it felt like my prize.

After a night spent on the concrete floor of the lab, I was ready to sleep through what remained of my Sunday. Before taking a shower and climbing into bed, I thumbed through the "A" s in my notebook of alphabetized plant remedies, looking for ayahuasca, the remedy in question. It wasn't there. Then I realized that Don Rodrigo never called it that. In his world it was referred to as *La Medicina* or the tea ceremony. Paging further, to the heading La Medicina, I found what I was looking for, the notes written several months back. As I read the words, it was as though Don Rodrigo was speaking them.

You must pick the chacruna leaf at sunrise in a special way. First you say a prayer and thank Mother Nature for her gifts. Only pick the lower leaves from each tree, choosing no more than twenty leaves from each tree.

Next you scrape the bark from the caapi vines with wooden spoons, gently and carefully pulling all the mulch away from the roots.

Beside that phrase I had pasted a rough sketch of the heart-shaped vines.

Next you pound these pieces of vine with a wooden mallet until the fiber is softened. Layering the leaves and the fibers from the vine in a large cooking pot, cover with water.

Cook over an open fire for several hours and allow to cool. Then strain the mixture into a separate container until only the liquid remains.

I closed my eyes, trying to remember those early days, when my teacher and I rose at dawn and made our way down the path that took us deep into the forest searching for the chacruna's shiny green leaves.

"Dad, can you help me out? I need you to look something up."

"Sure, Carrie. But I thought it was easier for you to get online now that you're a little closer to civilization."

"I know, but even here, sometimes the internet connection is slow, especially when everyone gets online at the same time."

"OK, I'm all ears."

"There's a San Francisco start up called Eureka Pharmaceuticals. It's run by a woman named Roz Becker."

"Writing it down now. OK, got it. What do you need?"

"Everything you can get – like when they started, who are their officers, how much money do they have. Any projects they are working on."

"I'll take a look and see if I can find out if anything's been written about them. Like press releases and stuff like that."

"Thanks Dad."

"When do you need it?"

"Now, please?"

Fourteen

Someone called my name. "Carrie, Carrie." Then knocking. I rolled over. "Maria, that's OK. I don't need housekeeping today."

The tapping continued. "Carrie, it's me, Margo. Get up. Didn't you see my note? We're doing yoga this morning, next to the falls at 7:30."

"OK, OK Margo. Give me a sec." I checked the clock. A few minutes before seven. *What day is it? I didn't see any note, but I'd be up for some exercise. Maybe, a good way to calm my nerves.*

Sitting on the bed, events of the last two days careened through my brain. *In Mel's fantasy, he hoped to engage Don Rodrigo in a scheme to manufacture ayahuasca. Then there was the night spent I'd sleeping on the lab floor, and then watching Mel fly out over the jungle in a two-man helicopter. Too much.*

"C'mon be a pal. I need bodies." Margo waited outside. "James is letting me give yoga a try. If it works and people like it, I can do it a couple times a week and he'll give us a break off the cost of our room. C'mon."

"Just a minute." My stomach rumbled. "I'll get dressed and grab some coffee. Meet you there."

I threw cold water on my face, brushed my teeth and dug my ratty gym clothes out of a drawer. No yoga mat, so I grabbed a towel on my way out the door.

The breakfast buffet called out to me but there was no time even for coffee. Instead, I followed a newly painted sign that pointed to the falls, the location of James' most recent project. The freshly built wooden deck, complete with bar, was constructed in hopes of attracting wedding parties and other events to the lodge.

Beside the path, plants glistened from an overnight rain. Hanging from a tree, a sleepy-eyed sloth munched a mango plucked from a tree in Gloria's organic garden. Tended with love and devotion, the plot supplied the greens, beans, peppers, tomatoes, and tropical fruits to the lodge kitchen. Soon, the roar of the Seven Sisters Falls filled my ears. Ever the environmentalist, James daydreamed about harnessing the cascade of rushing water to create an energy source for the lodge bearing its name. Someday he might make it happen.

Gloria waved me over and I plunked down next to where she sat, dressed in t-shirt and tights. "I'm so excited," she said. "I love yoga and it will be fun doing it in a group. It's so much better than just watching a video and doing it on my own."

I had to agree. "It feels like years since I've been part of an exercise class or any other type of organized social activity, for that matter," I laughed, trying to make a joke of it. But sadly, it was too true. I guessed Margo had an ally with Gloria providing some help convincing James to open up the new deck for a morning yoga class.

Reassured by the friendly faces of Gloria, Margo, Ellen, and Josh, I was glad I'd gotten out of bed. Looking around, I decided that my own shabby outfit wasn't as bad as I thought. Ellen had opted for sweats and a t-shirt instead of yoga gear. Josh was looking tall, lanky and cute in his cut-offs and a tank top. Seated with eyes closed, he didn't seem to care that he was the lone male of the gathering. Maybe he was used to it. The California students had spent much of their summer at the lodge, the three of them camping out in the one small bungalow.

Dappled sunlight filtered through the palm trees. When a morpho butterfly landed on a bush nearby, it took me back to the first time I'd seen the blue wings of the brilliant butterfly. One my first trip to Belize, our group of students was sitting at the outdoor café in San Ignacio when the butterfly landed for the briefest second on my sleeve. Even as it quickly flew off, the moment felt like a small miracle.

We all settled in on our mats and towels. As I counted heads, there were a few guests I didn't recognize and one that I did. Roz, in designer yoga wear, sat quietly, her eyes closed, back turned. I knew who she was, but she hadn't seen me and now I could let myself stare, confident that she would be none the wiser.

After some minutes of meditative breathing, Margo quietly suggested that we thank ourselves for the morning's practice. "Set an intention for yourself today," she said.

What might my intention be? That was an uncomfortable question. *Clarity? Direction? Connection?* Instead of counting my inhales and exhales, I felt the words hang in the air above my head. I was at a loss.

As we ran through the sun salutation, I managed to put that out of my mind. After the third downward facing dog, I snuck a peek at Roz. She took the poses easily and I was envious of her fluidity. I often did a bit of solo stretching in my room, to loosen up, but it had been a long time since I'd seen the inside of a gym.

As Margo guided us through a series of strenuous twists, I

was glad for the thatched roof over the deck. Even with the breeze coming off the falls, the morning sun was growing stronger and we were working up a sweat. Gradually, the poses became less vigorous and the class finished with some gentle stretching followed by a heart opener.

Sitting in a final meditation, my inner voice asked, "Why are you here?" For the second time this morning, I had no answers. Early on, during my first years in Belize, my goals had been so clear, just like the crystal water that now coursed over the falls. All that had changed somehow. Now everything was muddy. "What now?" I asked myself.

The sound of Margo's voice intoning "namaste" brought the class to its conclusion, but I had no answers.

Ellen, Josh and I hung out, guzzling bottled water from the bar, waiting for Margo to finish chatting up the guests who surrounded her. She responded to their appreciative comments about the class, "Thanks so much. If you'd like more yoga, be sure to tell James you enjoyed it."

From the corner of my eye, I watched Roz grab her belongings and move toward the path that led back to the lodge. Whispering to Ellen that I would catch up with them later, I trailed Roz, keeping my distance. As she slowed her pace, I wondered if I should approach her with small talk.

Instead, Roz turned abruptly. "Great class, wasn't it?"

"Yes, the class was in luck. Margo is an experienced teacher," I said. "Perfect location, too. Here by the falls."

"Are you here for vacation?" she asked.

"No, I've been here in Belize for a while. Working on a project."

"Interesting country, isn't it?"

Before I could answer, Mel appeared at the top of the path, almost as if summoned by an evil spirit. "Roz, I've been trying to reach you. Did you get my message?"

"Good morning, Mel," Roz said.

The he saw me. "And Carrie. This is a surprise. I didn't know you two had met."

Roz turned to me, "Oh, so you're Carrie?"

"Yes, the young scientist I was telling you about," Mel said.

"So lovely to meet you, Carrie." She offered her hand, and we shook briefly before she looked back to him. "Mel, I must say this is convenient. I wondered if you and I would have a chance to talk today. My colleague, Jeff Donnelly, arrives this afternoon. I want you to meet him."

"Jeff Donnelly?" I felt my brain explode. "Do you mean the Professor Jeff Donnelly from University of Illinois?"

"Yes, you've heard of him?" Roz asked.

Heard of him? "He was my advisor in graduate school. I first came here to Belize as his student."

"Small world." She smiled, looking pleased with herself. "We'll be having dinner here tonight. Of course, you must join us."

By the time I escaped from Mel and Roz, yoga's calming effects had worn off. My insides were heaving, and my breath came in anxious gulps. *Jeff? Eureka Pharmaceuticals? Really?*

Stumbling back to my room, I mulled over my time spent with Jeff. I remembered the first time I walked into his class. Tall and youthful, with wavy brown hair and a beard, he looked more grad student than professor as he perched on his desk at the front of the lecture hall. As he regaled us with stories of his expeditions down jungle rivers through the rainforest, I wondered if he was aware that half the class already had a crush on him?

Early on, between my junior and senior year there was the "for credit" field trip he led to a country I'd barely even heard of. After that, my plans for med school took a back seat. As a grad student, I'd enrolled in the ethnobotany department where he was assistant department head. The faculty advisor on my thesis, he'd been someone I was eager to stay close to, someone I'd counted on as a source of encouragement. Out on my own, that first year after graduation doing research in Belize, we'd kept in touch via email as I updated him on my progress. But once I'd moved off the grid, to be closer to Don Rodrigo, communication became difficult and we'd lost touch. But now what?

In a panic, I called home. "Dad, what did you find out?"

"Check your email for the documents I sent. They're the financials on Eureka Pharmaceuticals. Looks like a pretty new outfit but the CEO, Roz Becker has some history. Her background's in finance. She started out as a consultant for Arthur Andersen. After they folded, she went out on her own. Her first company, a start-up, sold a plant-based product, taken internally that was supposed to repel mosquitoes."

"I wonder what it was?"

"Dried lemongrass mixed with something else, I forget what. Unfortunately, it took too long to work. Then they made it into capsules. Those were not popular either."

"That's a common remedy here. It's easy to grow, plentiful and cheap to produce. Maybe not fast-acting enough for city folks."

"There were other ventures after that one, like a plant-based remedy they found in Brazil that was supposed to combat intestinal problems for people taking HIV drugs. That one did OK in the clinical trials but didn't garner much acceptance by the medical community. FYI, this Roz has already taken one company through bankruptcy. So, this is her second go-around. Last year they applied for an NIH grant but that fell through. You'll see the hype about something called bioprospecting in the articles I sent you."

"Yes, Dad. I know what that means They steal plant knowledge from the indigenous people and sell it for profit. Now I guess they're back to try something else."

"Carrie, take a look at what I sent you and let me know if you need anything else. Will you have time to do it today?"

"Yes, I'll have time. I won't be going back to the lab for a while." Until I knew what was happening, I was staying put, right there at the lodge.

I had to find a way to speak with Jeff, to find out what was going on with him before dinner. Was it possible that he was knowingly a part of this? Or had he been duped into a crazy scheme like I was? I had to find out.

If I tried to wait for him in the lobby, I might run into Roz and that would not be cool. I wondered if Gloria might tell me which room Jeff was be staying in. Or would he be sharing the large suite with Roz? *God, I hope not.* I didn't like to think about the implications of that.

I went looking for Margo and Ellen by the pool. "What are you guys up to?" I asked.

"I plan to write up my notes from yesterday's trip to the dig at Caracol. I'm way behind," Margo said. "I think Josh is putting finishing touches on some of the drawings he needs to go with the article he's been working on all summer."

"Ha! Call me the conscientious one," Ellen crowed. She made a face at her roomie, Margo. "I already did my notes last night while you guys hung out in the bar."

"Good job, Ellen. Do you want to play detective?" I asked.

"You know I do. I'm getting fairly good at this. Who do you want me to spy on this time?"

"I want you to hang out in the lobby and be on the lookout for any new check-ins." I flipped open my phone, pulled up Jeff's picture and showed it to her. "Keep an eye out for him and see if you can find out his room number. As soon as he gets here, let me know."

"Very cute. Who is he?" she asked. "An old crush?"

Yes, but I'm not gonna go there.

"No. He was my academic advisor in grad school."

"And he's coming here to see you?"

"No, he doesn't even know I'm here, but I need to talk to him. It's urgent. You remember what I told you about Mel? The guy in the dining room the other night? And the blond woman, Roz?"

She nodded..

"Somehow my advisor, Jeff is connected to her. I don't know what his role is, but I need to find out."

"Carrie, trust me. I'm on the case. Go sit by the pool and relax. I'll keep an eye out. That's what friends are for."

Fifteen

Scrolling through my photos later, I found a favorite shot of Jeff and me. This was the Jeff I knew, the beard, the plaid shirt, with rimless spectacles perched on his nose. It was taken the day my dissertation got approved. Glasses raised; we'd gone out together for a beer to celebrate. The joyful expression on my face, a reminder that I'd always felt myself bloom in his presence. Life felt so simple then.

Mom would have been pleased to see me looking so well-groomed. I'd claimed never to pay much attention to my looks, but I remembered trying that day. Styled for the benefit of the doctoral committee, my dark auburn hair was smooth and shining. And judging by the picture, I'd even worn a little eye make-up to bring out the color of my hazel green eyes.

Would I recognize Jeff now? Would he recognize me? Was it only three years since we'd last met? No, it felt like much longer. When he was my advisor, his ideas were solid, and I took them as gospel. Still, I wondered, what could be going on with Jeff now for him to sign on with someone like Roz. That was hard for me to imagine. *Surely, he couldn't have changed that much.*

I'd saved some of the emails Jeff and I traded that first year I was in Belize. They were enthusiastic, excited and full of details about my pursuit of Don Rodrigo. In them, Jeff offered guidance from his own days spent studying with a village shaman in the Amazon. It was from him I'd first heard of these traditional healers and how their work was in danger of being lost. When I wrote him that Don Rodrigo wasn't eager for my help, he told me not to give up. He advised me to assist the old man any way I could, even if it meant helping him do the farm work. I'd taken his suggestions, plowing the fields and weeding the garden. And he'd been right. It worked. Don Rodrigo finally agreed to let me join him. As I reread our messages back and forth, I became nostalgic both for the Jeff that I knew and the eager, excited version of myself who shone through in those words.

I caught sight of myself in the mirror. *What would Jeff think?* Most likely, he'd laugh when he saw me, say I'd "gone native." I took a second look. He might be right. My wavy hair was a tangled mess, and it could use a shampoo. When was the last time I'd had it cut? There was that one trip to the small beauty parlor in San Ignacio that Gloria recommended. The stylist did a fine job, but that was months ago. Since then, I'd hacked at it myself and it showed. Even worse were the hands I held up in front of my face, nails, ragged and grubby. I remembered the manicure set Mom gave me the last time I was home. Did I still have it somewhere?

No word from Ellen yet. She'd promised to hang out in the lobby and let me know if anyone who looked like Jeff turned up. Too curious to stay in my room any longer, I decided it was time to go investigate. With a scarf over the messy hair, I hoped no one would notice me. Entering through a side door, I spotted Ellen, sitting near the main entrance, sound asleep.

Sliding behind her chair, I gave a lock of her blond hair a gentle tug and she jumped. I bent over and whispered in her ear. "See anything?"

She looked around, sheepish. "Oh, Carrie. Sorry. I must have just dozed off. Nothing so far."

Spying Gloria at check-in, I went to the desk. "Gloria, I could have sworn that I saw an old friend arrive, Jeff Donnelly. I waved but couldn't get his attention. Were my eyes playing tricks on me?"

"Oh, you know Dr. Donnelly?" Gloria said. "Yes, he checked in about an hour ago. You might be able to catch him at the pool. I heard him say he couldn't wait to dive in."

"That sounds like Jeff. Thanks, Gloria."

I found Ellen. "OK, Sherlock Holmes, you're off duty. He's here. Gloria told me where to look for him. I'm going to the pool."

"Do you want me to go with you?" she asked.

"Thanks, but I have to do this one on my own."

Back in my room, I pulled on a bathing suit and went in search of my ex-professor. There he was poolside, engrossed in a book, nose slathered with zinc oxide against the strong tropical sun. I sauntered to the empty lounge chair next to him, grateful there was no Roz in sight. Trying for casual, I spread a towel and stretched out, waiting for him to look up from his reading. Moments passed.

"Hello, Jeff."

At the sound of his name, he jumped, almost dropping the book. "Carrie? Carrie Mullen? Can it be you? I wondered if you might still be in Belize. But I didn't expect to see you right here."

"I guess I could say the same. How are you?"

"Feeling great right now. That ride up Mountain Pine Ridge was more than a little bumpy." He rubbed his spine. "I forgot how bad the roads are. I guess that hasn't changed, has it?"

"Well, there has been some talk of building a runway in the jungle to make it easier for tourists to get here by plane, but that hasn't happened yet. Anyway, it's great to see you. At dinner tonight I'd really look forward to catching up."

"Love to but…" He trailed off, looking embarrassed.

"You've already got plans. I know. Believe it or not, I've met your friend, Roz. Seems like she's in the middle of a negotiation with a mutual connection, Mel Powers. He and I have been working together, as well."

"You have? You're kidding."

"And since you and Roz are meeting with Mel tonight, she invited me to join all of you."

"That's amazing. I want to hear about that but first, fill me in. I want to know what you've been working on."

"Do you remember all those emails, I wrote you? My first year here in Belize was a little rough. I spent most of it chasing Don Rodrigo, following him around, trying to convince him to let me work with him. At first, he didn't want to hear about it. You probably don't remember giving it, but I followed your advice. I helped him plant his corn and tend his garden. Once he saw I was a hard worker, then he listened. From then on, he accepted me, and I spent many months with him in the forest."

"Carrie, I'm proud of you. You're living the dream."

"Yes, I was. But like all dreams, you wake up. Things were going well until they weren't. Don Rodrigo claims to be ninety. He must surely be older than that. He's really not sure what year he was born. But now, sadly, he is ailing. When his family moved in to take care of him, I saw that it was time for me to leave."

"It's kind of crazy that we find ourselves here. It seems like you and I are both at a crossroads," Jeff said.

"Yes, my head is spinning. But, please, you've got to tell me how your partnership with Roz came to be. What about the university, your teaching, your family?"

The cheerful look faded. "Not a great story," he said. "When the school lost a good portion of their state funding, the fiscal belt tightened. First of all, the regular student population dropped. On top of that, the school lost a lot of foreign students who were paying full tuition and then some. You know, it's all about the demographics. After that they shrunk the department."

"You didn't quit, did you?"

"Hell no, I'd be crazy to quit when I have tenure. No matter what, it's a state school. They'll always have to find a place for me somehow. What I decided to do was take a sabbatical and see what other options were around. I thought maybe I'd look for some grant opportunities or consulting gigs. That's when I met Roz at a conference. She was doing a presentation about the strategy for Eureka and I have to say her plans wowed the conference attendees, me included. The business model calls for Eureka to connect with traditional healers for the purpose of uncovering viable plant remedies they have been using."

"Does that sound like stealing to you?"

"I can see how some might think that. I felt the same when I first heard of the bioprospecting business plan. But Eureka Pharmaceuticals is creating a way to promote conservation of the tropical forests. At the same time, they hope to build a bridge between the needs and practices of the indigenous cultures and the rest of the population."

"That sounds like propaganda taken right out of their promotional literature."

"Maybe it does. But honest, I didn't write it. As for Roz, we're not partners. She brought me on board as a consultant. That's my story in a nutshell. But tell me more. What about your research?"

"It's right here." I pointed to my head. "You can't imagine all that Don Rodrigo taught me. I watched him heal hundreds, no thousands of patients. We spent so many hours and days in the forest. He taught me to identify hundreds of plants. Where to find them, what they look like, how to prepare them, how to use them for different conditions. Most importantly," I pointed to my heart, "he taught me how to heal."

"I want to hear everything."

"Unfortunately, I couldn't stay at Don Rodrigo's farm any longer but, I still wanted to stay here in Belize. I had hopes of buying some land, setting up an herb farm similar to what I'd worked on there. When I got caught up with Mel on the rebound, it seemed like working with him would be a way I could do it."

You are truly…"

"Jeff…Jeff. How's the water?" Roz waved from her balcony. "Save me a space. I'll just grab my suit."

"I better go," I said. "But I'll see you tonight at dinner. By the way, are you staying in a cabin or at the main lodge?"

"Second floor, here at the lodge. Room 28. Why don't you stop by later and we can catch up?"

Dinner was scheduled for seven thirty. Checking my wardrobe was useless. Even with clothing my parents had sent as gifts, I had nothing presentable to wear for a social occasion. And it wasn't like I could make a trip to the mall, there wasn't one. At three o'clock, desperate for something to wear, I went to the cabin that Margo and Ellen shared with Josh. As I described my situation and my utter inability to cope, somehow, I managed not to cry.

Even though Josh was used to "girl talk" he suggested that I might feel more comfortable if he went for a hike. I thanked him. Once he left, I begged my friends, "You've got to help me. I've been in the jungle too long. All I have are grubby looking black pants and an old denim skirt that needs a wash."

As Ellen stood next to me, we gazed in the mirror at our lopsided reflection, "I don't think I'm the right size," she said. I was several inches taller and a few pounds lighter. "But Margo, I bet you have something Carrie can wear."

Margo pulled out a coral-colored sundress. "This might work," she said, holding it up next to me.

"It's so cute. Let me try it." I tore off my t-shirt and slipped the dress over my head.

Ellen gave a thumbs up. "It fits you perfectly."

"You're welcome to wear it," Margo said. "It's a good color for you, too."

"But what about this mop." I pulled at my hair.

"You are in luck," Margo said. "Back when we lived in the dorms, Ellen was the resident beautician. She used to give everyone haircuts."

"Ellen, I'm game if you are."

"Bring it on! Before we get stared, go in the bathroom and dunk your head under the faucet. Your hair will be easier to cut when it's wet."

"If you want shampoo, there's some in the shower," Margo said.

Hair dripping, I returned with a towel around my neck. "Where do you want me?'

"Sit here," Ellen commanded. I watched her arrange a pair of scissors, a hand mirror and a comb. She rubbed her hands together. "I've been wanting to do this for a long time."

"I don't know how much to cut," I said. "What do you think?"

"I say we get rid of a good six inches." She held the damp locks between two fingers, letting me see what six inches might look like. When I nodded agreement, she began to comb through pulling at the tangles. Starting from the back, section by section, she began to cut. The hair fell in clumps to the floor. By the time she progressed to the sides, I was liking what I saw. "Bangs?" she asked. I shook my head no.

Margo dug into her bag and produced a beautiful tortoise shell hair clip. "You can borrow this. It'll hold the hair off your face." She demonstrated. "See how good it looks? Now you can see your eyes."

"All that's missing is a little eye shadow, some mascara and some lipstick." Ellen applied the necessary make-up. When she was done, she held up a hand mirror. "See what I mean? When you look good, you feel good. Now take this for later." She pulled out a few cosmetics, handing them over.

As I looked in the mirror, a smile played around my lips. I gave each of them a hug. "You guys are the best. Thanks so much. You saved me from total embarrassment."

A mirror hung near the stairs on the second floor of the lodge. Catching a glimpse of myself, I was more than pleased with my new haircut, the dress and the make-up. It all produced the desired effect and I looked like a grown-up. Happy with what I saw, I allowed myself a second look before I knocked on the door of Room 28.

Jeff answered, looking groggy. "Carrie, come in. I must have conked out. Forgot how tiring this tropical sun can be."

"Should I come back?"

"No, now's a good time. Wow, you look great."

A blush of pleasure crept over my cheeks.

Jeff's room was small, nothing compared to Roz' spacious suite. But it opened out to a lovely little balcony with just enough room for two chairs.

"Go on outside," Jeff said. "It's a beautiful evening."

I found a chair and watched the birds soaring on an invisible current of air high above the tree line.

"Are you thirsty?" Jeff asked. "Let's see what's in the mini-bar." He found two soft drinks and brought them out. For a moment, we sat silent watching the palm leaves sway.

"So, your man, Mel. What's he like? I read a few old articles about him in the Wall Street Journal. And Roz seems impressed. Fill me in. How long have you known him?"

"Not long. Just a couple months, although it feels like longer. When you meet Mel, he comes on strong, plenty of stories to tell, plenty of ideas. You'll hear many plans but don't take everything he says at face value. Trust me, I know."

"I met a couple guys like that at a venture capital seminar. Same deal. That was a learning experience."

"Don't be surprised if Mel changes course on a dime. Our first project was to be a plant-based antibiotic. He'd gotten a grant from the Belize government that included guarantees to hire local people as part of the project. He and I outfitted a lab complete with refrigeration, drying equipment and more. Before the first procedure was even underway, he'd moved on. Once he met Don Rodrigo and saw his healing first-hand, any work on the antibiotics morphed into something completely different. Still not sure what. But he and Roz were discussing ways to produce ayahuasca. I heard them talk about growing the plants in green houses and then trying to create the formula in pill form. After that, clinical trials."

"Whoa!" Jeff looked stunned.

"I just wanted to give you a heads-up."

Jeff checked his watch.

"Better let you get dressed," I said

Sixteen

Rain might be on its way, but for now, the doors to the veranda at the Seven Sisters Lodge were thrown wide, welcoming the evening breeze. Standing by the open door, I gave myself a minute to get my bearings. Inside, the dining room buzzed with activity. Waiters hustled, bearing trays laden with food and drink. On the far side of the room, James, the owner, presided over the bar. Polishing a glass with a white towel, he leaned in to listen to a customer, then threw his head back in hearty laughter. I wished I felt like laughing, but I didn't. My chest pounded and the top of my head tightened in a grip of anxiety. My father's words, spoken during our last phone conversation, echoed in my brain. "You can always come home," he'd said.

Yes, Dad, you're right. I can. I'm fortunate, I can turn tail and run, leaving this crazy country behind. Luckily, I have some-where to go and at age twenty-eight, time is still on my side.

But what of all the research I've done with Don Rodrigo. What about all the time we'd spent working together? Right now, I felt like time was the enemy and I didn't know how much time my teacher still had. In addition, my work, the legacy of his wisdom and skill might be at risk around people like Roz and Eureka Pharmaceuticals. In the company mission statement, bioprospecting was just a fancy word for finding, using and profiting from the resources of the rainforest and its people.

I remembered several grad school lectures on the European travelers. who came to the New World and found plants that produced the chocolate, potatoes, coffee and other crops. The plants, shown to them by the indigenous people, became vast sources of wealth harvested from the Caribbean and what is now called Central America. There was a quote that struck such a chord that I'd made sure to write it down somewhere. "Plants may seldom figure in the grand narrative of war, peace, and even everyday life but they are often at the center of the intrigue."

Just as indigenous people then were treated as sources to be exploited and eliminated, that same rapacious mindset still exists today flourishing under the free enterprise system exemplified by companies like Eureka Pharmaceuticals.

Over in a corner, I spotted Mel, Roz, and Jeff seated at a table for four, an empty chair waiting for me. I saw Jeff check his watch and scan the room. I'd purposely timed my arrival ten minutes after the seven thirty reservation, to make sure Jeff would be there before I arrived. As he waved me over, I wondered if he would be an ally? Time would tell. But no way could I have faced sitting there with Mel and Roz without him.

"Hey, Carrie." Jeff pulled a chair out so I could squeeze in. The conversation was well underway.

As usual Mel's voice was drowning out anyone else. "Roz, tomorrow, how about you and Jeff take a field trip? You can both come to my place to see the compound. Afterward, Carrie can show you the lab. We can also take a look at the other piece of property that I was telling you about."

"Tomorrow would be a great time to visit your site, Mel." Roz said. "My chemist, Greg Kramer, is flying into Belize City tonight."

"Carrie, hear that?" Jeff said. "We're going to get a look at your lab."

Had the lab and my role as "young scientist" become props in Mel's play? My hand went to the small silk pouch at my throat. Inside it nestled the tiny jade amulet. I'd learned that the fetish, given to me by Don Rodrigo, symbolized self-reliance. Now I wore it to remind myself of what I was there to accomplish.

Earlier, an idea occurred to me and I waited for the right time to share it with my dinner companions. But conversation was diverted for a couple of minutes when the waiter appeared, and we ordered drinks.

I turned to Mel. "Early on, you and I talked about other plants that have many therapeutic possibilities. A natural antibiotic might have a good chance for approval by the FDA. But, right now, ayahuasca is classified as a Class A Narcotic. While there are a couple of churches in the US who have permission to use ayahuasca as a sacrament in their religious practice, it's outlawed for everyone else. Right out of the gate, it would be fighting an uphill battle."

Roz's face showed her displeasure, but I plowed on. "I'd like to suggest that we start out with a different remedy. One that Don Rodrigo has used for years."

"What are you referring to?" Jeff asked.

"It's called sorosi by the local people."

Mel's eyes lit up. "Hmm, didn't we talk about that one before?"

"It's been used as a cure for diabetes."

"Did Don Rodrigo ever mention anything that would cure herpes?" Smirking, Mel hit the table with his hand. "For sure, there's a market for that in the States."

As I shook my head no, it was all I could do not to roll my eyes.

"Carrie, any other curative plants with multiple uses come to mind?" Jeff asked.

I rattled off the popular names of three or four of Don Rodrigo's most used plant cures, secure in the knowledge that there was an adequate supply of plant sources. These were plants I'd seen used safely and with good results.

Drinks arrived and Mel held up his glass. "Let's drink to a new partnership. Eureka Pharmaceuticals and Mother Nature."

We clinked glasses all around. Roz took a tiny sip and placed her cocktail back on the table. "Jeff, what's your take on this?"

"As you know, Roz, plants themselves are not patentable. And Carrie has a good point with the FDA issue. So maybe try something else instead of the ayahuasca, something that won't be such a tough sell."

I could see she didn't think much of Jeff's comment.

"Still, I'd like to meet with Don Rodrigo," Roz said. "Carrie, I wonder if he would agree to an interview?"

When I felt Jeff's, foot tap mine under the table I wondered if that was merely a random movement or a communication from Jeff to slow things down. *Jeff, are you my ally?*

"I'll be happy to help you connect with his nephew, Julio. He's become Don Rodrigo's apprentice. But why don't we all visit Mel's set-up first. I can't wait to show you the lab. I have samples of some of the plants on hand. And we can discuss the ways they're used."

"I'd like to suggest that we also consider sourcing questions." Jeff turned to Roz. "Do we harvest these plants in their natural habitat? Do we pay others to do so, do we grow them ourselves?"

"Good point," Roz said. "I'm sure these are some of the issues that our chemist, Greg, will want to discuss."

Mel cut in. "There are about twenty acres of available land right next to my site. Most of it already cleared. A real estate developer's plan went belly up. He's looking to unload cheap. I've already talked to him once. The site includes a couple of buildings, almost finished."

"It's a nice piece of property," I said. "A lovely little spot on the river."

"Yeah, it's close to a water source and there's room for cultivation," Mel said. "And let's not forget the other plan I talked to you about Roz. There's no law against using ayahuasca here in Belize. We can always go back to our earlier idea; setting up the therapeutic retreat here in Belize to help the wounded warriors suffering from PTSD."

Before we finished dessert, Mel promised to send his Jeep for us the next morning. Leaving the restaurant, Mel asked me if I could arrange a meeting with Don Rodrigo.

"I'll see what I can do. He hasn't been feeling well lately." Sadly, that was true and even if it weren't, I'd already made up my mind to keep Roz as far from the old shaman as I could. Dinner was over and Mel and Roz went off to greet her chemist who'd just arrived and was checking in. Breathing a sigh of relief, Jeff and I stepped outside on the veranda with our drinks. The clouds had passed over and the moon was bright.

"Have you seen the Seven Sisters Falls?" I asked.

Jeff shook his head, "No, but I'd like to."

"It should be beautiful there tonight. Let's go see. I could use some air. It'll cool my thoughts," I said.

"Lead the way," Jeff said, throwing a friendly arm around my shoulders. We walked in silence for a few moments until he turned to face me. "OK, Carrie. Something's bothering you. I get it. You don't like Roz and you don't trust Mel, but they're not doing anything that other drug companies haven't already done."

"But Jeff, that doesn't make it right. That first field trip you took us on after my junior year made a big impression. Wasn't it you who first told me about Don Rodrigo? Until then I was on my way to med school. Do you remember?"

"Sure, I remember but I never expected that you'd take it this far."

"Take it this far? It's good someone did. Trust me, there was little written documentation on the traditional healers in Belize, but when I started working with Don Rodrigo, I realized this was a chance to change that. So, I made notes, a couple hundred pages of notes, collected plant specimens. Otherwise, it seemed like all that knowledge would be lost."

"I'd love to see what you have. How many pages did you say it was?"

"I didn't. I'm not really sure at this point."

"Before Roz came on the scene Mel was gung-ho about setting up a therapeutic retreat for combat vets with PTSD like Ronnie."

"Ronnie?"

"Yes, he came to Belize to work security for Mel. Just recently he participated in an ayahuasca tea ceremony at the compound. It really helped. Once Mel saw how it worked, he came up with a plan to set up a retreat for vets with Post Traumatic Stress Disorder so they could get that same ayahuasca treatment. Maybe that's still an option or maybe it will just become another one of Mel's schemes that have fallen by the wayside. Anyway, we'll see what happens tomorrow."

"I want to keep Roz away from my mentor. Until now, Mel was focused on the ayahuasca retreat. I hoped he and Roz would agree on that as a viable project. You can help make that happen. I read about a spa in Costa Rica. They do a weeklong treatment and a charge fee per client. It could be a real business and it could also help people. If you can convince Roz that there's money to be made there, we can easily use those plants and take some of the pressure off her efforts to steal whatever she can from the legacy of people like Don Rodrigo."

We reached the end of the garden path. To change the subject, I pointed out a colorful array of orchids James had planted. At the sight of the falls bathed in moonlight, Jeff caught his breath. We stood, transfixed.

Jeff didn't speak for several minutes. Leaning against the wooden railing, he turned to face me. "OK, I see your point. I could propose a plan to cultivate and produce something other than the plant material used to make ayahuasca, but I don't know if they'll buy into it." He ran his hand through his hair, a gesture I'd always found appealing. "Yes, and tomorrow is tomorrow. We'll see where it goes."

The water rushing over the falls mirrored my emotions. "Tonight feels crazy, doesn't it?"

"Yes, it does. For now, let's forget about business. Let's start over," Jeff said.

Falling silent, we gazed at the water coursing over the rocks. "Did you see that?" he pointed. "That fish jumping out of the foam, right there?"

When I turned too late to see it, my foot twisted, throwing me off balance. As Jeff grabbed my elbow to steady me, our eyes locked. His lips curved into a smile, softly cradling the side of my cheek, he drew me to him. "I've been wanting to do this all night," he said. Closing my eyes, I let the moment happen.

In the dark of Jeff's room, my eyes snapped open. He was still sleeping. I brushed his hand with my lips and sat up. Retrieving Margo's dress from where it landed on a chair, I pulled it over my head and grabbed my shoes. Tiptoeing to the stairs, I was careful to avoid the hall mirror.

Alone in my room, my heart burned in my chest. I knew that I still felt the same about Jeff. No different than the minute I clapped eyes on him that first day in his classroom.

Whatever that feeling, love or hero-worship, I didn't want to feel it anymore. Standing under the shower, I let the tears flow while a soft voice told me what I already knew to be true. I would never be more than a ridiculously small part of his life.

Seventeen

Jeff, Roz, and Greg Kramer, the Eureka chemist, took in the scenery as Ronnie, silent behind the wheel, maneuvered the unpaved dirt road heading west from the lodge to Mel's compound. Roz kept her cool but Greg, the new arrival, wasn't used to the physical realities of Belize transportation.

"Are all the roads in Belize like this?" Greg wondered after we cratered a third time.

"Welcome to Central America," I said. "Unfortunately, the answer to that question is probably yes."

"Looking forward to seeing your lab, Carrie," Roz said. "Jeff mentioned that you were one of his students. We'll see what he taught you." She elbowed Jeff in an effort to be playful, but I could see his face redden before he turned to look out the window.

The gate to the compound stood open and Mel stood waiting on the veranda. "Welcome. Welcome. Great day for a walkabout." Our first stop was the gazebo, the outdoor space constructed for the first ayahuasca experiment.

Though the day was not yet hot, my underarms were damp, and my stomach was in a knot.

Next stop on the tour was the lab. Poking around, Jeff looked impressed. First, he inspected the refrigerator and then the drying unit. "I'll say this, Carrie. You have some state-of-the-art equipment here. Just what you need for plant processing."

Roz looked bored. "Very nice. Jeff, I'm sure you have some questions."

"Have you processed any plant samples yet?" Jeff asked dutifully.

"We identified several compounds that could have antibiotic properties, but we're still deciding which of these plants will be our focus. Mel and I talked about screening them for bioactivity, but we didn't get beyond that yet."

"There's a video I can show you. Interesting," Mel said. "In it, I talk about identifying some important cures. It was shown on Belize TV."

The day Don Rodrigo visited the lab was so different. There was a feeling of comfort as the old man puttered around. Curious, he picked up Bunsen burners and looked inside petri dishes and puzzled over the drying oven. Afterwards, he'd offered prayers, chanting as he smudged the newly built structure with burning herbs, to give it his blessing. It reminded me of the connection we shared. Since then, the lab had stood empty and now I noticed spider webs in a corner.

"Too much research, not enough action," Med said. "That's why we decided to concentrate on the "wounded warrior" program."

"The what?" Roz asked.

"The Wounded Warrior effort. That's what we're calling our initiative to treat vets with PTSD," Mel said. "And Ronnie, the guard who drove you to the compound, he was our first test case."

"Test case?" Jeff asked.

"Ronnie served a couple of tours in Iraq." I said. "He's a good man but, a while back, it became obvious that the poor guy was suffering classic symptoms of PTSD. He was having flashbacks, feeling threatened. It was getting tense."

"Yeah, the police were here," Mel said.

"On the day he came to bless the lab, Don Rodrigo befriended Ronnie and was helping him to deal with his fears. Later, he suggested to Ronnie that the tea ceremony could bring him lasting relief. And it really helped. I'm sure Ronnie can tell you how the experience changed him."

"Interesting," Roz said.

"Once we hit on that therapeutic concept, we spent more time preparing for a location and getting ready for the first ayahuasca ceremony," I said.

"Where did you get the plant material?" Greg, the chemist, addressed Mel for the first time.

Mel turned in my direction. "Carrie, you and your assistant, Julio took care of that, didn't you?"

"Yes, the plant material for that was collected in the forest and prepared at Don Rodrigo's farm."

"Let's go visit him," Roz said. "I'm sure he's a gold mine of information."

Visit Don Rodrigo? Did she think she could just barge onto his front porch, and double talk the old man into handing over a lifetime of work? Who does she think she was dealing with?

"Wait, first I want you to take a look at the parcel of land I was telling you about," Mel said. "It's just down the road. Other side of the fence." He pointed. "Then we can have lunch."

Roz groaned.

"What's the matter?' Mel asked.

"I'm sure it's an interesting parcel, but it's really beside the point." Roz said.

Mel's brows knit together in dismay, but for a change, he stayed quiet.

It was almost noon by the time the jeep pulled up the gravel road past the fading signage for Palomar Estates. The two sample homes stood forlorn in the middle of the open tract of land surrounded by forest and bush. I remembered promotional brochures strewn around the lodge. They promised a swimming pool, tennis courts, and a fun, ex-pat lifestyle for snowbirds seeking a second home in the tropics. Sadly, like so many other developments fading at the edge of the jungle, there had been no takers. There would be no Palomar Estates.

Mel jumped out of the jeep, charging onto the porch of the sample. "Come on," he beckoned. "This is where we could bunk the retreat participants. I figure there's room to sleep four in each unit. Beds, bath and a common room. That makes for eight participants, four in each house. Maybe a basketball court or some other sports opportunity here. A place to blow off steam. Meals and any group sessions all would take place at the main compound, of course. The rest of the land can be fenced off for greenhouses to grow the plant material or whatever."

He motioned to Ronnie, behind the wheel. "Ronnie, you're our target market. Tell us what you think of this idea."

Ronnie nodded, "I like it."

"Why ask him?" Greg muttered under his breath.

"Ronnie is our one-man focus group," Mel said.

"How much do they want for the land?" Roz asked.

"Trust me. It's a steal," Mel said.

"And if you buy it, then what?"

"Come inside. Take a look."

Jeff went along with the program and stuck his head in the door of one of the unfinished houses for a brief look. Feeling detached, I stood nearby, watching in the shade. As the others wandered away, Jeff found a moment for us to be out of earshot. "Carrie, about last night. I'm sorry...I don't know what..."

"No worries..." I dug my nails into my palm, trying to hold back tears. "We're friends."

Before he could say more, Roz was back, "Carrie, how many acres did Mel say this property includes?"

"I think it was twenty acres or so."

"OK, maybe the rest of the acreage could be cleared, fenced off. I wonder if it could be used for greenhouses to grow the plant material," Roz said.

"Why not?" Mel said.

"Great," Roz said. "I have something I want to run by all of you before we even get started. It's something I'm calling the Shaman Apprentice program." She turned to Mel. "We can talk about it over lunch."

Gabrielle put out a lovely spread of sandwiches and fruit, but I wasn't hungry. For many reasons, it wasn't a good day.

"The Shaman Apprentice program is a win-win for everyone, the people of Belize, Don Rodrigo and his family and of course, Eureka and its shareholders. Through incentives, we create a school for the local people." Roz turned to me. "We bring in healers, like your shaman."

Another scheme to get to Don Rodrigo? Of course.

"The native healers teach the young people, keeping the traditional knowledge, the plant wisdom of the Maya people alive. Every few years or so, we select a likely candidate, someone with potential, who has absorbed the most knowledge. We award that lucky young person a scholarship. And Jeff, here's where you come in. Eureka will subsidize the education of this candidate at your university and in your department. You'll be their sponsor, their mentor. What do you think?"

"Who would these young apprentices be?" Jeff asked. "How would you find them?"

Roz turned to me. "Does your teacher have young relatives who would be interested?"

"That's a painful subject for him," I said. "His nephew, Julio, has become his apprentice Unfortunately, the other young people, those who haven't already left to find jobs, don't have much interest."

"Maybe some sort of stipend would change their mind?" Greg said.

"I like it," Mel said. "Maybe I should run this concept by my contacts with the Belize Department of Economic Development. They are always looking for a way to create jobs." He turned to me. "Julio was grateful for the work when he helped you set up the lab. After that he learned enough from his uncle to perform the tea ceremony. Maybe we should talk to him, see if he would be interested."

"Can you call Don Rodrigo?" Roz asked.

"He doesn't have a telephone. Doesn't have electricity."

Eighteen

The day felt like it would never end. Roz frowned her displeasure, but for now, the old man was safe on his small farm, safely hidden away, beyond the only road in his village. Maybe I could offer to introduce her to another local healer, Doña Luisa who lived nearby in San Miguel.

Then Greg had a suggestion. "The guy who drove me from the airport last night talked about a guy in this area who helped his sister fight off an infection. Said he's an herbal doctor who's cured a lot of people. His name is Gilberto Reyes, and he has an office in a town called San Ignacio."

I knew of Gilberto. He had a good reputation and was considered knowledgeable, but unlike Don Rodrigo, he didn't gather or grow his own herbs and plants. He took a less hands-on approach, purchasing dried plant material or hiring some of the local women to go into the forest and gather plants for him. He'd treated many people here in town if they didn't have the wherewithal to get to Don Rodrigo.

"It's not too far from here," I said.

Roz reluctantly agreed to seek him out and we headed into San Ignacio in search of Senõr Reyes. Luckily, he wasn't hard to find. A sign, with his name was visible from the street. It read 'Jungle Remedies: Diabetes, Prostate, Cancer.'

His office was on the first floor of a two-story frame house painted a soft shade of yellow. Beyond its bright blue door, a woman sat at the front desk, presiding over a room full of people waiting to be seen. Roz, of course, had no plans to sit and wait. As I watched, she murmured to the receptionist as she slipped something into her hand. After a brief delay, we were ushered into the small examination room. Roz and I grabbed the only two chairs, while Mel, Jeff and Greg crowded in behind us. As we faced Gilberto across the desk, my eyes were drawn to a shelf of small, glass bottles filled with colorful liquids.

"And to what do I owe this honor?" asked Reyes, looking surprised at the group before him.

Roz introduced herself, mentioning her company and its mission to seek new plant-based healing remedies. "And what shall we call you, *Senõr?*" She asked.

"You can just call me Gilberto," he said, in unaccented English. Reyes nodded politely as she explained her goal of working to support the rainforest and the indigenous people of Belize. "I'd like to hear more but first, tell me, how can I help you?"

"Gilberto, tell us about yourself," Mel decided to hurry things along. "When did you begin to treat sick people?"

"Going back many years, I learned everything from my grandparents," he said. "They came here when Belize was still a British colony. It was nothing but jungle then, not even access roads from the coast to the larger towns or the capital. There was only one doctor in the whole area. If you could get to see him, he charged a lot. When people got sick in those days, they relied on plants to get healed. Many people still do. I've never seen a doctor in my whole life. And look at me." As he stood and puffed out his chest. I thought he looked ready to thump it, Tarzan style.

Roz gave him an encouraging nod. "Do you have a special cure you can tell us about?"

"The types of diseases I've been known to cure are high blood pressure, HIV, hepatitis. I also have treatments for gallstones, kidney stones, and heart disease. If you have clogged arteries, I could give you a treatment to clean them. No surgery."

Mel pointed to the shelf full of remedies. "Tell us about those bottles of colored liquid behind you. How do they work?"

"You'd be surprised. People often come to me after everything else fails. I get letters asking me to sell my products and I do. I mail all over the world. I've cured thousands of people over the last 30 years, including some who have full blown AIDS. I've had stories written about me in the newspapers. But don't take my word for it. Look at these testimonials."

From a drawer, he produced an overflowing three-ring binder. Shuffling though the pages, he pointed out one well-worn letter from New York, then another. "Here's one from Los Angeles, he said, pulling out paperwork. I saw the attached envelope did have a California post mark. "Read this."

Roz glanced briefly at the well-thumbed page, while I read what I could. Written by a man named Alex, the letter praised the mail order remedy he'd received from Gilberto. He believed it helped to restore his health; giving him a much-needed burst of energy after painful bouts of chemotherapy.

Gilberto tapped the letter as if to prove a point. "Alex was a tough case, but the remedy helped him enjoy life again. He even sent a letter about it to a fellow from the National Cancer Institute in Washington, DC. Told him how he was helped."

"Let me ask you a question," Mel said. "Do you ever treat people with the tea ceremony?"

Gilberto shook his head. "You mean ayahuasca? No, I leave that to the shaman. They get help from the spirits. I just count on what my grandparents told me and what I've learned from the plants."

"Very nice," Roz said moving on. "We wanted to tell you about a new project called the Shaman's Apprentice Program. It's designed to appeal to young people in your community, to help them learn more about traditional medicine. We thought you might be interested."

Gilberto nodded and listened.

"We want to recruit young people in this area and teach them the basics of traditional healing. There would be a stipend for those who complete the course and other rewards as well. Do you think any young students nearby might be interested?"

Gilberto's eyes lit up. "Of course. Especially if there's a chance to earn some money." He pointed to a flyer on his wall. "When you mentioned that Shaman's Apprentice idea, it reminded me of the Traditional Healers Conference. They'll be holding it at the Belize Ecology Park. Here, let me show you something else. I've had letters from some foreign nurses and even doctors, too. They're planning to visit me here, next summer."

Just then, the receptionist knocked on the door. "Gilberto, there's an emergency outside. Snake bite," she said.

"Sorry, folks. Here's my card if you want to contact me," Gilberto said.

Heading for the door, we filed past a young boy clutching his arm, his face wet with tears. My heart went out to him, but Roz didn't blink as she stepped outside.

"He's might be a useful contact but, he's not right for us," she said.

Back at the lodge, Roz claimed a headache, and went straight from the car to her suite. Soon, Mel took off back to his compound. Outside the lodge, I was surprised to see Julio waiting for me near the lobby door. There was a line across his brow that I hadn't seen before. I motioned him away from the veranda where he was waiting. "Quick, let's go around back. We can talk there," I said. I wanted to keep him away from trouble.

Silently we picked our way down the gravel path toward the sound of rushing water. "Julio, you look worried. What's wrong?"

"My uncle he is asking for you."

"You should have called me. How is he doing?"

"When he sleeps in the night, he calls out for his wife, for his daughter, but you know they are both with the gods." He pointed to the sky.

"What can I do?"

"Come with me now," Julio said.

"I don't want Mel or anyone to see us together. You go get the car, drive out by the front gate and I'll meet you down the road in a few minutes." Julio gave me a puzzled look but went back to the car.

I ran back to my room to grab my bag and use the bathroom. On my way back, Jeff turned up. He grabbed my hand, pulling me closer. "Carrie, I have an idea," he said. "Do you have time for a drink?"

His breath was warm on my ear, my arm tingled. His touch left me shaken. "I'd like to talk now, but I have to be somewhere."

"OK, I'll talk fast. I was thinking that maybe you should consider sending your files to the university."

"Why would I do that?" *I thought he wanted to talk about us.*

"Well, it's your alma mater, too. Think about it. You'd be sending them to me. Maybe we could work together, create a repository, set up a research project, maybe get a grant from the NIH. What do you think?"

How does he know about my files? Then it came to me. After too much wine, I'd told him all about them.

Was it just last night that we'd stood together in the

moonlight? Why had I done that? I wanted to blame it on too much to drink, but when he'd asked me questions, I was transported back to being the student, hoping to impress him.

"There's not really that much there. If the NIH wanted to do some good work, they could send a team here and help me record the knowledge before it's too late."

"You know, I also have a colleague who got a contract at NIH. We connected at a conference not too long ago. Maybe I can send him an email. What do you think? His name is…"

"Jeff, if you asked me about this a year ago, I would have said yes. But now, you're on sabbatical. Under contract to Roz and she's breathing down my neck. Sorry, I have to go."

"Will I see you later," he asked.

"I'm not sure."

"Come find me," he said, promise in his voice.

I'd already hidden all my notes and samples in a box under the bed. I vowed to come up with a safer place for them. For now, I was determined to disrupt any attempts of Roz, Mel and company to use Don Rodrigo for their purposes.

Beyond the Seven Sisters gate, Julio waited around the bend. The moment I jumped into his car, I felt more protected. Julio hit the gas, and the tires spun out, throwing up grit. I felt relief as we left the world of Mel, Roz and Eureka Pharmaceuticals behind.

Don Rodrigo sat alone on the porch. Leaning over a chopping block, his hands shook as he tried to slice bark from a branch of the copal tree. There was a tiny nick on his thumbs that was bleeding. I gave him a clean tissue from my bag, and he pressed it against his thumb until the bleeding stopped.

"Let me do it." I dragged a stool over near where he sat and held out my hand.

He handed me the knife and for some minutes I silently

chopped away at the sweet-smelling bark. Finally, he spoke. "You have always been my good helper, my good student. You have learned all that I can teach you."

"I'll never know all that you know. Even now, whenever I visit you, I learn something new. Now tell me what's wrong."

"Last week I had a dream. The Maya spirits appeared to me. I heard them speak. They said, we see that you are working hard, but you are old and tired. I think they are right. I am ninety years old and I am dying soon."

"No, no! Don't say that. It's not true."

"And today, I woke up with a terrible *dolor en mi estómago*. The pain in my stomach, it started this morning."

"Show me where it hurts and let me make you a poultice."

He took the hand I offered, allowing me to draw him into the house and lead him to his bed. As the old man gingerly stretched himself out on the narrow cot where he had slept for so many years, I went to the stove and warmed castor oil. When it was ready, I dipped a cotton towel in the oil, placing it on his mid-section.

"Let this warm your belly," I said. "See if you can sleep."

I went outside and sat on the porch, my head in in my hands. When Julio gave me a searching look, I tried to shake off the sadness with activity. Placing the copal bark shavings in a pan, I poured water over them. "The tea is good for stomach pain," I said.

Julio and I sat quietly on the porch waiting for the tea to cool. When we heard groaning, I went back inside, and moved the oil compress. "Where is the pain?" I asked.

He pointed to where his abdomen bulged in a way I hadn't noticed. As I had seen him do many times with his patients. I moved my fingers around the upper edge of the pain.

With a groan, he expelled some gas. "*Gracias*. I feel better now."

"Good, now try to sit up a bit and drink this tea I made you from the copal bark." After a few sips from the cup, he closed his eyes and rested.

"He seems a little better. He's resting," I said. Julio and I sat for several minutes until there was a cry.

"*Mi hija*, come quick."

"What's wrong?" Again, I ran inside, fear clutching my chest.

"I want to tell you something. I am not afraid to leave this world behind," he said. "But I want to be relieved of my sins."

"Sins? *What could he have to confess?* What sins?"

"When I was a young man, I worked in the chicle camps harvesting the gum. When it was payday, I was no good. I drank a lot and never came home to give my wife the money. In those days, I slept with many women, but my wife never knew. But I never slept with a patient. I would never do that."

I held his hand and tried to soothe him. I was surprised but not shocked. This was not the Don Rodrigo that I knew but his behavior in his younger days was no different from many other men of his time. "I'm sure your wife would forgive you. And think of all the people, thousands of them, that you have helped."

"My wife, she, too, came to me in my dream. She told me it is not my time yet, but soon."

"You are not ready. You still have many gifts. Now finish the tea and you'll feel better."

"Thank you, my friend. I feel better already. You have given me strength. I remember when Josefina told me not to trust you. She said your interest in me was not good. But she was wrong."

There was a knock on the door. A young villager stuck her head in. "Can Don Rodrigo help me?"

"No, I'm sorry. He's not seeing patients today."

At the sound of a female voice, I heard movement from the corner. "Who's there?" he asked, lifting the curtain from around the bed.

"It's me, Elena from the village. Can you help me?"

He looked past me to where she stood at the door. "Of course. What is your problem, *Mamacita?*"

The color had returned to his face. Don Rodrigo threw his arms up. "Now I feel better."

With a smile, he ushered Elena inside. "What ails you, my child? I cure high blood pressure, arthritis and broken hearts. I've been doing this work for many years and I can help you."

Why was I surprised?

Gesturing a welcome, he smiled at the young woman. "*Adelante,* come in."

Nineteen

The next day, I called Julio from my room. "How is Don Rodrigo today? How's he feeling?"

"He said he slept good last night. And this morning he was hungry enough to eat two tortillas and some rice."

"That's a good sign. His stomach must be better. How is his mood?"

"I would say he's up and down."

"I have an idea that might help cheer him up. Julio, are you free tomorrow?'

"Daytime?"

"Yes." *I forgot what day it was. Best not to interfere with Julio's Saturday nights.*

"I think so, why?"

There's a meeting at the ecology park. I wonder if your uncle would like to go to it."

"What is it?"

"A gathering of traditional healers from all over Belize. What do you think?"

A pretty, young woman in a long Mayan skirt and an embroidered blouse waved us in at the gate of the ecology park. Don Rodrigo waved back, motioning her to him from his open window. "Tell me, my daughter, are you a healer?'

"*No, Señor,* I'm just helping out. My mother is one of the people in charge of the meeting today."

"Your mama? What is her name? Perhaps I know her."

"Margarita Vargas. That's her over there, helping them arrange the tables for food."

She pointed to a tall, dark-haired woman in glasses, directing the setup amidst a swirl of activity. If I was surprised by the diversity of the crowd, I shouldn't have been. Like any country in Central America, Belize is a product of its history. The people in the western part of the country, near the Guatemalan border, are a mix of Mayan and European bloodlines, tracing their ancestry and their language from the days of the Spanish conquest. They often speak a mix of Spanish, English and Q'eche´, the Mayan tongue. The people from the Belize Caribbean coast track their origins to immigration, voluntary and otherwise, from Africa and the West Indies. The healers from that coast speak a mix of English and Creole. Today, several of those present were dressed in colorful African-print clothing.

It was an exhilarating sight. Julio had barely managed to park before Don Rodrigo spoke up. "Let me out," he said, opening the passenger side door. Energized, the old man was ready to join the throng. Fearful he might fall, I walked close to him as he made his way, leaning on the stick he'd brought for support.

With Julio on one side of his uncle and me on the other, we moved slowly through the crowd. Margarita Vargas turned to watch our progress. She waved to the old man, making her way to his side. "Welcome, *Señor.* We are honored to have you with us. I am so glad you got our invitation,"

"Invitation? No, *Señora.* I don't remember it. But, *gracias.*" He looked pleased.

Julio and I exchanged looks. At best, Belize mail delivery is difficult. Post offices are few, and the mail might or might not make its way to the village grocery store near where the old man lived. Even if it were delivered to him at his farm, he might well put the letter away for safekeeping only to forget its existence before anyone could read it to him.

A bell sounded and *Señora* Vargas urged everyone to find a seat. We followed the others into the rough-hewn park building. Inside, there were rows of chairs for the audience and a raised table at the front set up for a panel. As we found seats on the aisle, several people turned to greet Don Rodrigo. The recognition was a tonic to his spirits. Bright-eyed, my teacher sat up straighter and looked around with interest, smiling and waving to those he knew.

Speaking first in English and then Spanish, Margarita thanked the Belize government for their participation. Once she'd introduced the panel of Mayan and Creole healers, a tall dark-skinned man in a navy blazer walked to the microphone. Introducing himself as a representative of the Belize Office of the Economic Development, he welcomed everyone to the meeting. I hadn't known that the Belize government was partnering with the traditional healers, but their sponsorship was a good sign.

"Before we begin, I'd like to introduce two distinguished visitors from the United States. They are here working with the National Institute of Health in Washington, D.C."

He pointed out two young Americans in the front row, one male, one female, giving their names. As they stood, I scrambled in my bag in search of a pen and felt myself sit up straighter. The conference, already motivating, became even more interesting.

Then *Señora* Vargas asked everyone to honor a special guest, the most respected healer in Belize. When she named Don

Rodrigo, he looked at Julio in surprise. As the room burst into applause, he pointed to himself as if to say, 'who me'? A huge grin played across his features as Julio helped him to his feet. "*Gracias, gracias,*" he murmured, his head nodding in acknowledgment.

I was so glad we had come. The warmth and energy of those in the audience felt like a gift. Even though the many young people shrugged off the ways of their elders, the Belize government seemed to be ready to acknowledge the value of those gathered here today. After working for so long in isolation in the remote forests of western Belize, it was easy to be overlooked, and difficult to make connections with the outside world.

The first issue on the agenda was forest preservation. To loud applause, *Señora* Vargas gently reminded the audience and the minister that the growth of ecotourism in Belize made saving the country's natural resources even more important. She volunteered that the members of the healers' association were eager to act as guardians of the natural habitat. "In return for our help, we ask that the government set aside acreage and funds to safeguard the natural resources and keep them safe."

A passionate audience offered up anecdotes that described some of the more egregious abuses. They labeled the loggers, the ranchers, clearing land to graze cattle, the poachers, and the drug cartels as adversaries.

"The forests, once destroyed, do not return," said one of the panelists. Across the room, the audience shouted their agreement. Acting as eyes and ears, they would make the government aware of what was going on in the remote corners of the country.

A nurse spoke about the new-found interest of students from North America and Europe who were coming to Belize to learn about non-traditional medicine. "College students, healthcare practitioners and naturopathic healers are eager to learn more about the natural plant remedies to be found in Belize," she said. "I am proud to say that our country has become known for its healing traditions."

As the discussion continued, I felt a weight on my shoulder. Looking down, I found a sleeping Don Rodrigo slumped at my side. At the lunch break, I woke him gently. He blinked, looking around in surprise. Finding himself surrounded by his fellow healers, he soon regained his bearings. Many wanted to introduce themselves and to ask for his blessing. Others, old friends, he hadn't seen for ages, came in search of hugs and conversation. As the guest of honor, he was thrilled to be the center of attention. My heart filled with joy and I could almost see the years slipping away.

Lunch outside was a colorful affair of music, crafts, and food. Culinary selections included burritos, tamales, fried fish, and conch soup. The hearty menu was accompanied by singing, drumming, and even some dancing as the Creole healers from the coast played drums and shook rattles. Under a group of trees, the gentle strains of Mayan reed flutes could be heard above the drumbeats, adding an ethereal sound.

After lunch, Don Rodrigo's energy again began to flag. He whispered to Julio that he was tired and ready to go home. Before he took his uncle back to the car, Julio assured me that he would do his best to return for me at the end of the day. But I knew it was Saturday, Julio's night to perform at the café in San Ignacio. It was the highpoint of his week.

"That's OK," I said, glad for the cash in my wallet. "I'm pretty sure I'll be able to find someone to give me a lift back to the lodge."

At the afternoon break, I sought out the two American scientists from Washington. They told me that they had been in Belize for some weeks, working on a grant to identify and collect plant samples with active healing potential.

"Wait a minute. Is your name Carrie?" the female member of the team asked.

Surprised, I nodded and held out my hand, "Yes, Carrie Mullen."

"I'm Debra and this is Brad. We heard about you from Jeff Donnelly. He said you came here to study, but since he hadn't been in touch for a while, he didn't know if you were still here."

"You won't believe it, but Jeff is here in Belize now. He's doing a consulting job with a pharmaceutical company. He's staying about an hour's drive from here. Where are you?"

"We're at a hotel in San Ignacio," Brad said. "We've got to get together after this event is over."

They supported the healers hopes of convincing the Belize government to set aside designated land as a study center for medicinal plants and healing. "Do you think there's a chance the Belize government would set aside land like Margarita Vargas suggested?"

"Money pressures in the poor countries of Central and South America are pushing down on the natural world. For the people of Belize, the loss of the pristine forest, is exactly like what's happening in the Amazon," Debra said.

"Is there any chance that the U. S. government could help?" I asked.

"Washington is still digging its way out of the financial slump from the market crisis in 2008. The federal budget is tight. But some of the wealthier foundations are looking at the climate emergency in the southern hemisphere," Brad said.

The Americans, sorry to have missed their chance with Don Rodrigo, peppered me with questions about the work I'd done since coming to the country. Their immediate goal was to create a list of plant species most widely used by the healers of Belize. I felt safer in discussing my work with them. They felt grateful to Margarita Vargas for holding the meeting that allowed them to connect with all the healers they'd met today. They were a formidable group. While they might be isolated by their remote location and a lack of resources, together, there was real strength in the knowledge they shared. That power sustained them.

When reporters and a TV camera crew appeared to record the closing ceremony, I was sorry that Don Rodrigo left early. I would have loved to see him on TV. Although some indigenous attendees hung back from the press, Margarita did not. Moving quickly, she engaged with a Spanish-speaking reporter.

I was surprised when one of the reporters from the English language station stuck a microphone in my face, so I decided to follow her lead.

"Tell the viewers what plans your group has for moving forward," the reporter asked.

"We're hoping that the Belize government will consider allocating a large tract of land for the preservation of the forest. It's important for the traditions of the people of Belize but also, the world." Was I speaking for the group or myself? It didn't seem to matter. The cameras were rolling.

Twenty

The next morning, I spotted Mel prowling the grounds of the Seven Sisters Lodge and he waved me down. "Where were you yesterday?" he asked. "I tried to get in touch all day."

I swallowed a smile knowing I'd kept my phone turned off for that very reason. Still, I knew he'd left several messages. "Maybe my service was down. I was at a conference for traditional healers. You know there isn't much cell phone coverage out there in the bush."

"A conference? Carrie, why didn't you tell me? Maybe Roz and I would have gone with you." Mel sounded irritated.

"It wasn't a secret. I heard about it when we went to see Gilberto and so did you. Don't you remember the flyer he had on his wall? No one seemed interested. So, Julio and I took Don Rodrigo. Good thing we did. Turns out he was a guest of honor."

"Did you take notes, record anything?"

I shook my head. "There was a TV crew there. I didn't have a chance to see if it showed up on the news. There was a discussion on setting aside state-owned land for cultivation of healing plants. A lot of rainforest is being lost, especially thousands of acres in the south. Apparently, the government finally noticed, and they are offering to help the people."

"Oh, OK," Mel said, losing interest. "I get it." Conservation wasn't one of his hot buttons. "I want to run something by you."

"I'm listening."

"I made a bid on the land we looked at, the old Palomar Estates property. Fairly sure they're going to take the offer. I'm meeting them there today."

"Congratulations, is Roz partnering with you on that?"

"The deal, working with Roz is still in the "maybe" stage. So, we'll see where that goes."

"Then what's the next step?"

"We go ahead with our original plan and set up the first ayahuasca/PTSD retreat. Get the two buildings in shape. Think about promotion. Oh, by the way, your friend Jeff left."

"Jeff left?" My heart plummeted. "What happened?"

I was only gone one day. Why didn't he call me?

"Did he leave any word?"

Mel shrugged. "His wife called. One of his kids was in a car accident and she wanted him to come home."

"Will he be back?"

"I doubt it. Roz didn't want him to leave. They had a big blowup. So, he just quit."

Don't cry. Don't cry. I dug my fingernails into my palm. *Nothing you can do.*

"I'm so sorry I didn't hear of that. I would have tried to talk him out of it before he left."

"I don't know if you could. It happened pretty fast."

"You just said you needed my help. What do you need me to do?"

"I want you to spend some time with Ronnie. Get him talking. Hear what he has to say about our PTSD experiment with ayahuasca. He was our one-man focus group, remember?"

"How has he been, overall?"

"He's been a lot calmer, no more incidents."

"That's good news."

"Yeah, so I want you to talk to him about his experiences with ayahuasca. Write it all down. Maybe take him to see Don Rodrigo. Let the old man do some more of his healing work. We want Ronnie to be our spokesperson for the PTSD project."

Mel confirmed there was a budget for this and when he promised to have a check waiting for me tomorrow, I agreed.

I could use the money, my monthly bill for room and board at the lodge sat, unpaid, on the dresser in my room.

I hadn't seen much of Ronnie since Roz and company arrived. Of course, there was the time he'd spent behind the wheel of Mel's jeep, chauffeuring us around the countryside. But we hadn't talked much.

Ronnie? A little rough around the edges but basically a good guy. For sure, he's easy on the eyes, but how would he be as a spokesperson? Maybe I should get Julio to work with me on this. Ronnie and Julio have definitely bonded. And Julio always needs cash.

That afternoon, I called Julio to tell him of Mel's plan. He took me up on the offer and we agreed to meet the next morning. But for now, there was time to kill. My friends were off exploring, but at least the day was clear and sunny so, left to my own devices, I got through the rest of the day by swimming laps in the pool. As I toweled myself off, I only hoped I'd be able to sleep.

Later, I lay awake, in the darkness, my thoughts teeming. *What did you expect? It was only one night. No promises.*

The words of my father buzzed in my head. *You can always come home.*

Come home, really? "It's not too early to start thinking about the holidays," he'd said the last time we'd talked. It was almost November. "Do you want me to get you a ticket?"

I thought back to the last few times my folks sent me airline tickets and I flew home for the holidays. It was great to see my family, and, to give them credit, they didn't pressure me or try to convince me to change my goals. December in Chicago is cold, windy and gray and being there made me nervous. To pass the time, I connected with friends, learning who had gotten married, who had babies, who finished advanced degrees or started big jobs. They'd been living their lives while I, machete in hand, chopped my way through the jungle with my favorite nonagenarian.

A few hardy souls, my parents included, assured me they'd fly down one day and visit Belize for a vacation. I always promised a warm welcome but so far, no one had taken me up on my offer of hospitality. Back home, after a few days spent stuck indoors with the Christmas tree, I remembered how happy I was to return to the jungle and my work with my teacher.

Finally, I fell asleep.

The next day, Julio and I drove out to Mel's place for our first interview with Ronnie. As the ex-soldier came out to greet us. I had to agree, Mel was right. He looked better, stronger, calmer. Even his color looked healthier.

"Looking good, man," Julio said as he and Ronnie high fived. "Great to see you."

Watching the two of them chat, my anxiety eased. "Mel told you why we're here?" I asked. Ronnie grinned, nodded and opened his arms as if to invite me in. As we hugged it out, this new connection between us felt like a good start to our conversation.

Mel appeared to greet us, shaking hands with Julio and clapping him on the shoulder. I was glad to see that Mel treated Julio with more respect.

It was pleasantly cool and breezy, the air scented with jasmine as Ronnie, Mel, Julio and I moved to the outdoor pavilion, the spot where we'd shared the ayahuasca experience some weeks earlier. When Mel went back to the house, claiming phone calls he had to make, it was time to begin. "Let's make use of the quiet," I said.

Mel had given Ronnie a small recorder to keep track of his thoughts and experience after that night. Ronnie held it up. "I love this little gizmo," he said. "It's a damn shame, the batteries are dead. But I can remember pretty much what I was feeling that night."

"Why don't you just talk, and I'll record you?" I held up my phone and Ronnie nodded.

"Let's do it, *amigo*," Julio said.

"I joined the military because of my uncle. He was a medic in the service, always talking about how he helped people. Growing up, he was my idol. I got along better with him than my own dad. He was a great guy, always with the stories so I wanted to be just like him. Right out of high school, age eighteen, I joined up. I wanted to earn a living, help people, maybe even get some money together for college, in case I changed my mind and decided to go back to school later."

"Like a lot of guys my age, I had plans. I wanted to serve, do something for myself and make my family proud. In my mind, I wanted to become a medic, and maybe, get trained for a career.

Instead, they assigned me to airborne ranger training and then sent me to the Middle East. I served three tours of duty, but never did get much in the way of career training. So, I satisfied myself by thinking that we were going to help the Iraqis, help them get rid of the bad guy, Sadam Hussein."

As time passed, though, Ronnie felt he'd been conned. "Looking back now, I realized that I re-upped because I didn't know what the fuck else to do. Somehow, I thought I would be the smarter version of a soldier. I got that wrong. I was doing more fighting than I ever could have believed, I felt like an idiot. I was a sucker. I didn't want to be the guy who was there to kill people. I know, I know," he said, throwing up his palms in a gesture of resignation. "You don't need to tell me. I was just a very green, very stupid kid."

"Sorry, man." Julio, silent until now, shook his head in sympathy.

"When I first got home, back to Florida, I was in denial. I didn't think I had a problem. Things there didn't look that different. Did I think I would I just go back to where I'd left off? Didn't happen, now I was drinking all the time, getting in fights. In fact, I bought a Harley and almost got myself killed. That's when I went to the VA hospital. They diagnosed me with PTSD, got me started on some therapy, and prescribed a bunch of anti-depressants which I didn't want to take. I didn't want to talk about it; didn't want anybody to know what I was going through."

"I was looking for a way out when I saw this job ad," he gestured toward the guardhouse. "It was on an employment website for former military personnel. 'Executive protection' it said. Wow! It sounded like just what I needed. If I got hired, I'd travel, be part of a small team, do some driving and maybe, do some investigation. The ad called for combat experience and a knowledge of Spanish. That was perfect. I had both and the pay was good."

"What was it about the job that brought out your stress?" I asked.

"Having to carry a gun again really bothered me. And Mel insisted we do target practice. And sometimes, the dogs barking drove me crazy, too."

"So that's how you felt before the tea ceremony," I said. "How did you feel afterward?"

"Calmer, a lot calmer than I'd felt in years. Most of the anger was gone. I felt like I could forgive what happened to me in the past."

"Maybe taking ayahuasca is not for everyone. I've heard some people, especially back home might get turned off by the idea that they'll vomit. Did that bother you?"

"Not much. I've been through a lot worse. It was kind of funny. I just felt like I was getting rid of a lot of negative feelings, like a cleansing. You let go of the anger, the hatred, the loneliness. Afterwards, I felt better than when I went to the therapist at the VA, I can tell you that."

"That feeling of relief, has it stayed with you?"

"So far."

"Any visions you remember from that night?" Julio asked. "Anything stick in your head?"

"It started off slow," Ronnie said. "I was feeling all these waves of warmth and light. Then the waves began to spread from my heart to my fingertips. I had this sense, I guess, you could call it, of love surrounding me. That dissolved my fears. I felt the call of the jungle, felt a connection to all the trees, the plants and the animals.

"When you get discharged, everything at home looks the same but you feel different. So, it's like, 'OK, what are you gonna do now?' But after the tea ceremony, it was like the welcome back I never had when I got back from Iraq. I felt loved," Ronnie said, tearing up.

Twenty One

Mel hired a crew of skilled carpenters to make alterations to the existing structures on land he'd just bought from a bankrupt real estate developer. The new parcel connected with his property and clearing a path through the forest would combine the two tracts of land. "It will be more like a campus, maybe even a resort," he said.

Could the retreat function as a resort, an overnight camp, or therapeutic setting? Or would it be a little of each? Basketball court, tennis court, some landscaping, an outdoor dining area, maybe, even a swimming pool or a hot tub? Two small houses already in place would be used like dorms, allowing the participants to walk over to the compound where meals, meetings and ceremonies would take place.

Digging a well, running water lines and connecting plumbing was another matter. Things that might be easily accomplished in a first world country, could be challenging in Belize. People still talked of the Christmas power blackout not so long ago, when a fire left the western part of the country dark for two days. I'd heard that things had changed for the better and now, existing power lines brought in electricity for close to ninety percent of the country.

Whatever the final plan might be, the crew of Mennonite carpenters Mel hired vowed they could handle it. These craftsmen were part of a community that arrived in western Belize in the 1950s. They were drawn to the country by the availability of land, seclusion, and the freedom to pursue their own religion and culture. In the years that followed, settlements sprang up. They cleared land, built homes, planted crops, and founded private schools for their children.

Though some in the group wanted a life of seclusion, word soon spread about the skills of the Mennonite builders. As demand for their workmanship increased, the light-haired workers in straw hats and bib overalls could be found building houses with lumber from their own mills. Members of their community who were more modernized gradually acquired some heavy equipment to make that work less challenging. Lucky for Mel, the group he hired even had a couple of diggers for clearing the land.

As the men worked on the project, the November weather cooperated, and progress moved quickly. Once the heavy lifting was done, outdoor sport and picnic areas were added to the space, and the two existing structures, built originally to be single-family vacation homes, were converted to four-person dormitories. I was glad there would only be eight available beds. That meant participants in the ceremony would be limited to a small group.

Mel turned his thoughts to promotion, and I wondered whether he would start running ads on the local TV and radio station. "No point in that," he said. "That's not our market. We're looking for folks who are into the latest trend, therapeutic tourism."

It was a term I hadn't heard before, but Mel must have been doing some homework.

Instead, he did outreach using connections from his days as a tech entrepreneur. He'd lost money in the crash of 2008 and his reputation had suffered after he fled the country to avoid damages in a million-dollar lawsuit that held him liable for an accidental death on his property. I was pretty sure that it was the lack of an extradition treaty between Belize and the U. S. was what brought Mel to the country in the first place.

Even with a cloud over his name, it seemed there were still reporters who wanted to know what Mel Powers was up to even if he'd been off the grid.

Mel kept a tally on his contacts in the press. He knew who he called and who called him back. When he mentioned a lengthy conversation with an editor at a major paper, I was skeptical, but soon after, he told me that the Miami Herald would be flying a reporter down for the day to interview him.

Before that day arrived, Mel wondered if Julio might bring Don Rodrigo to meet the reporter. When the old man declined as did his nephew, Ronnie and I were given our roles to fill that void. I was to be cast as a student of traditional medicine who could explain the mechanics of the tea ceremony and how it worked. Ronnie would be on hand to talk about the therapeutic results that helped him in his journey to overcome his own PTSD. Since what Mel requested wasn't far off base, I didn't see any reason to object.

Mel sent his car to the airport to collect the journalist who arrived on the early morning flight from Miami. I was pleased that she turned out to be a seasoned reporter working the Herald business desk.

"Great to meet you." She and Mel shook hands. "I'm Laura Hunter, beautiful place you have here," she said.

"It's coming along," said Mel.

Eyes wide open, she took in the security gate, the large house, the veranda, and the grounds. "Looks like you've carved some remarkable space out of the jungle. It's a nice break for me to be here. Wonderful change of scenery," she said. "Things have been pretty hectic in Miami. Belize feels very soothing."

As if on cue, Mother Nature provided some local color. A flock of green parakeets swooped screeching into a sour orange tree nearby.

"Thanks for coming down. I look forward to bringing your readers up to date," Mel said.

"I'm excited for the opportunity to learn about your new

projects. And I appreciate the chance to be here. You know the newspaper business has become a little rough." With a grin, the reporter pulled her shoulders back and rolled her head from side to side as if removing a crick from her neck.

"I hear you," Mel said. And we all laughed.

Ronnie quizzed the reporter about where she was from and how long she'd been living in Florida. Since Ronnie grew up in Miami, he looked forward to telling family and friends they would soon be reading about him in the local paper. "I can't wait for my mom to read it," he said. "Maybe it will make up for all the hard times I put her through."

Before Mel brought the reporter up to date on his new plans, he mentioned the initial grant he'd received from the Belize government to promote employment for the local people. For the second time, he used the phrase therapeutic tourism.

"Why would the Belize government give you a grant for that?" the reporter asked. "Just from what I saw on the drive here, the economic needs of the people seem vast. And isn't tourism one of the few businesses that are actually booming here?"

"In some parts of the country, that's true. A lot of cruise ships dock on the east coast, near the barrier islands. Tourists get off there and spend money. But luring tourists into the interior is tough because of transportation issues. So, in this part of the country, fewer tourists mean fewer jobs for the people. We want to change that. We'll be hiring drivers, cooks, cleaners, and others to support our facility. Right now, I've got four or five carpenters at work. You'll see what I mean in just a minute. I'm excited to show you how everything is coming together."

After lunch, we toured the compound, strolling down to the river's edge. Laura was delighted by the sight of three white egrets. As we watched, one of the birds bent its head into the swift-moving water in search of food and emerged with a wriggly fish in its beak.

The next stop on the tour was the lab. It had been sitting untouched for weeks. As my key clicked in the lock, the sight of a small green lizard scampering across the countertop gave me a start. Laura took a few photos of the lab interior and the equipment. "For background," she said. "It adds an interesting flavor to the story."

After that, we settled in under the canopy at the pavilion where the actual ceremony had taken place sometime before. "Aside from the ceremony itself, how important is the setting?" she asked.

"Carrie, why don't you answer that one," Mel said.

"Laura, I don't think I have to tell you that the world is a traumatic place and experiencing PTSD has become a part of that. In the U. S., the treatment involves psychological counseling and often a regimen of anti-depressants. Even if it's successful, that treatment is costly, and it can take years."

Ronnie spoke up. "I know. I went to the VA Hospital for counseling and took a million pills; but, trust me, it didn't work. That's why I'm here."

"That brings us to where we are at this point in time. So, while the demand for healing is high, not everyone is willing or able to find it. As word spreads about the tea ceremony and using ayahuasca, people want to experience it, and that's why some versions of the ceremony are taking place in cities around the world, usually in indoor locations," I said. "Many of those events may not be well controlled. It takes a lot of preparation, a positive setting, and knowledge. What we hope to do is to maintain a traditional approach by performing the ceremony in a natural environment," I said.

"I've heard about ayahuasca and its effects," Laura said. "What about the vomiting? Isn't that stressful?"

"Yes, that can be tough, no matter where you are. But being outside, in nature, provides a more relaxed healing atmosphere. It happens more easily when participants can move out into the surroundings to relieve themselves with a minimum of stress. In a natural setting like this, participants can freely release the effects of the initial purging that's part of the experience."

Laura scrunched up her nose. "To be honest, that might cause me to have second thoughts."

"It sounds worse than it is," I said. "Still, I understand what you mean. That's one reason we want the participants to be here on-site for at least five days ahead of time. Healthy meals are part of preparation for the ceremony. That means no alcohol, no red meat, and no sugar in the days prior. They can adjust to their new space and connect with each other and to our ceremony leader. They can have time to relax, participate in some recreational activities, and just enjoy nature."

"Who leads your ceremony?" the reporter asked.

"Our ceremony leader will be Julio Sanchez acting under the guidance of the well-respected traditional healer, Don Rodrigo Montoya."

"Ronnie has become close to Julio and Don Rodrigo. In fact, it was Don Rodrigo who first recognized and understood Ronnie's symptoms. Of course, he didn't call it PTSD; in his culture, it's known as *susto* or fear. He began treating Ronnie and has continued to provide ongoing treatment. Right, Ronnie?"

"For sure." Ronnie looked pleased to be asked. "All I knew was that I had a lot of anger stored up in me. I did three tours as a soldier in the Middle East, trying to prove something to myself and my family. The stress was non-stop. Afterward, I thought I could run away from it. But I was wrong. When I came here, I think I was trying to get away from myself," he said. "Once I got here, some of the bad stuff came back at me. After I got triggered by a flashback episode, I met up with Don Rodrigo, and he began working through the healing process with me."

"Thanks for sharing that, Ronnie. If I have a chance, I'd like to use that on the record if that's OK with you?" the reporter asked.

We'd walked through the forest, to observe the progress being made on the new tract of land. The foreman came over to shake Mel's hand. "Come take a look. We should only need two more days to finish." The carpenters, wearing the traditional denim overalls and broad-brimmed straw hats, proudly motioned us through the structures they were converting to dormitories.

"Really coming together," I said, breathing in the clean smell of fresh paint.

I had to laugh when I heard Mel ask the foreman if he had any experience installing a swimming pool. The foreman shook his head no. "But I might know someone who could do it," he said.

Overhead, the clouds grew dark and a strong wind bent the palm trees. As fat drops of rain began to hit us in the face. The carpenters, finished for the day, got into their truck and headed back out to the road.

"We better get back," Mel said.

"Before we go," the reporter asked, "I have one more question. What will you call this new facility?"

I could tell by the expression on Mel's face that he wasn't prepared for this question. Neither was I. It hadn't come up in our brainstorming sessions together. As if looking for answers, Mel spotted the faded sign for Palomar Estates laying abandoned on its side. "I'm considering several names, but for now, I like the "Palomar Project."

Back at Mel's house, as we waited for the rain to stop, he and Laura talked about his previous life as a tech entrepreneur. Her phone buzzed as a text came through, advising that her flight back to Miami was canceled due to bad weather. At that point, I suggested she might want to spend the night at the Seven Sisters. I was heading back there anyway. She and Mel shook hands, and Ronnie drove the two of us to the lodge.

Twenty Two

As we pulled into the car park, James, looking natty in a tropical print shirt and shorts, waved a welcome. Ever the host, he sprang to open the jeep door for Laura and I. "Carrie, how goes it? Haven't seen you lately."

"Could that be because you've been out campaigning?" I asked.

"You sound like my wife, Gloria. But yes, I guess you're right." He brushed a shock of straight white hair out of his eyes.

"Any progress?

"It's always a struggle," James said. "But we did have a productive meeting with the Department of Economic Development yesterday in the capital. A couple of Washington types, scientists from the NIH were at the table. That seemed to perk things up. There was talk of allocating land for a medicinal plant preserve. To sweeten the pot, the Americans dangled the possibility of funding for research on the designated land. They hope to identify the most effective species of healing plants. Oh, and by the way, they said they met you at a conference."

"They did? I'm thrilled they remembered me. I do have their contact information. I'll try to get in touch later."

"Meetings are great, but making a plan happen is always easier said than done. Still, it's a start. I'll keep you posted on the plant preserve idea," James said.

"Thanks, James. Say hello to Laura. She's a reporter for the Miami Herald, here to do a story on Mel's new project."

"Welcome, Laura." His expression took on interest. "Great to meet you. How long will you be here?"

"Probably just tonight. My flight home today was canceled due to weather."

"If you have a little time before you go, I'd be honored to tell your readers about the environmental situation here."

"I'd like to hear more." She checked her phone. "But if the weather calms down soon I'll be out of here by dawn tomorrow." Behind us, the high winds whipped the palms back and forth. More rain looked imminent.

"I have to see about a leak in one of the cabanas," James said. "Maybe we can talk later."

"Before you go, can I get an extra bed set up in my room?" I asked.

James hit his walkie talkie. Over the static, he asked his maintenance man to bring the folding bed.

"Thanks, James." I turned to Laura. "Now that you have a place to sleep, how about a drink?"

"OK, now you're talking my language. Point me to the bar."

"There's the door," I said. "Let's get inside before the rain hits again."

The lobby shutters were closed against the wind and the rain that was sure to follow. The flickering candles in the bar threw a warm glow that reflected off the polished wood interior.

"Oooh, this is nice." Laura said, a note of appreciation in her voice as we settled in. "Drinks are on me."

To go with the drinks, I ordered a snack of Mexican chicken wings, hot and spicy. They came with a cool, creamy sauce for dipping and a side of guacamole and chips. The weather had given us an appetite and we dug in.

"So, Mel?" Laura asked her raised eyebrows speaking volumes. "How is he as a boss?"

"With Mel you never know what the day will hold. Things change from minute to minute. When I met Mel, you might say I was on the rebound. My plans to stay in Belize had taken an unexpected turn. I needed a source of income and a place to stay. I'd been staying at a small herb farm outside the village."

"That sounds like an intriguing story. Tell me more."

"I came here originally to study traditional healing as its practiced here. I was fortunate to become a student of Don Rodrigo. It wasn't easy, but once he decided I was serious, we spent a few years together. During that time, I learned all I could. But sadly, his health began slipping. When his family moved in, I left."

Laura was an avid listener and so I spent the next half hour sharing my history, my years with Don Rodrigo, and the Mel connection.

"I'll bet I'm not the first person to tell you that you and Mel make an odd couple," she said. When my editor told me, I was coming here to interview one of the early tech legends, he hinted that Mel was here on the 'down low.' I'd read somewhere that after he sold the company, he got involved in some crazy schemes, he went a little loco."

"Yes, I'm familiar with Mel's loco side." We laughed as I recounted some of Mel's claim, early on, about a cure for cancer.

The television broke into regular programing to announce Breaking News. The handsome face of a young man appeared above the words, "Forest Ranger Killed by Poachers."

"Twenty-five-year-old Diego Colon, a self-appointed guardian of protected indigenous lands in western Belize, was found dead of gunshot wounds." The announcer continued. "Another volunteer ranger, Hugo Melendez, was wounded but managed to survive and is now in critical condition. What we know is that the two men came upon a group of loggers. According to the wounded survivor, the trespassers were illegally cutting mahogany and other wood on protected land." The announcer cut to a clip of a Belize official who stated, "If we want to preserve the benefits that the Belize forests can offer its citizens, we must recognize the people's rights to the land. We must protect it against intruders." Staring at the screen, I realized he was the same official who opened the traditional healers' conference I'd attended just days ago.

"Oh my God, James will be devastated by this." Were they friends of James, perhaps?

We finished our drinks as James ran into the bar. He'd already gotten word of the shooting. Making eye contact with Laura, he said, "This is the kind of thing I wanted to tell you about. Poachers, farmers, loggers stealing the wealth of the land set aside by the government. All the damage takes its toll, not just on the people of Belize but for the whole planet. It's the same here as in the Amazon. We need our forests to survive."

The news story upped the ante in Laura's eyes. Pushing exhaustion aside, she seemed more than ready to hear what he had to say. "Two stories for the price of one," she said. "My editor will like that."

An hour later, the reporter's head, notebook and cellphone were filled with stories of the environmental crisis in the country's rainforest, but her eyes looked heavy. Laura said. "I promise to pitch the story to my editor. I think he'll be interested," Laura said. "But I've been up since 4 a.m. I think I'm ready to crash."

We said our goodnights and headed into the darkness. Outside, songs of crickets filled the night air. The rain had already blown through and the stars appeared overhead. As promised, James had the folding bed delivered to my room and Laura lost no time climbing in. She gave a sigh of contentment, drifting off.

The next morning Laura was up before dawn to catch her flight back to Miami. When I offered to loan her anything she might need, she declined. "Thanks, Carrie, but I'm all set. I've learned never to leave town without tucking a toothbrush, make-up, and a change of underwear into my bag just in case."

Promising to stay in touch if there were any more questions pre-publication that needed answers, we gave each other a quick hug before Laura climbed into the shuttle that would take her back to the airport for her two-hour flight to Miami.

As I watched the van disappear beyond the lodge gates, my phone sounded. It was Julio. "Carrie, can you come soon? My uncle went out by himself early. I told him not to go, but you know he don't listen. When he slipped and fell on the trail, he hit his head. I don't know what to do. His friend, Doña Luisa is here, but he acts like he doesn't know her."

I begged James for a ride to the farm and I was grateful when he gave the maintenance man a nod to take me there. Both the driver and I cursed the ruts filled with muddy water that slowed us down.

Julio's sedan was parked next to the porch. The two small grandchildren chased each other around it, banging on the dented fenders and laughing until their grandmother, came out. "*Cállate! abuelo está enfermo.*" Be quiet, Grandfather is sick." Josefina scolded. "Here," she said, handing them corn. "Go feed the chickens." Running off, they threw the feed at each other as they chased the hens toward the vegetable garden.

The driver turned the Seven Sisters truck around to head

back and I waved him off. It might be that I'd have to find another way back later. But for now, I needed to be with my teacher. Slowly, I climbed the steps up to the porch. Inside, Josefina stood guard by the door, arms folded. Julio brushed past her and escorted me to where Don Rodrigo slept at the back of the house.

Don Rodrigo lay in his narrow bed, eyes closed, a compress on his forehead. Dried blood was visible below his temple. His arm, resting above the blanket, was an odd shade of purple.

"Tell me what happened," I said.

"He fell going down the trail. I knew it would be muddy from the rain. I told him not to go but he don't listen. When I heard a yell, I went after him. He was lying on the ground, his shoulder twisted up under him and blood coming from his head. When he fell, I think maybe hit his head on a rock."

Don Rodrigo's hand was cold. I touched his cheeks softly and gave his earlobe a tug. Gently I raised the old man's eyelid. "It must be a concussion. He needs to be awake, not asleep."

"Uncle, can you hear me?" Julio said, speaking softly into his ear.

"Where is Doña Luisa? You said she was here."

At that moment, Doña Luisa appeared, her arms filled with shoots of a flowering vine. "I found it, I found it!" She waved the large leaves overhead. "This will stop the blood," she said.

"I'm glad you found that" I said. I'd seen the plant before. The leaves were shaped like hooves and Don Rodrigo called it cowfoot. "There could be internal bleeding that we can't see."

At the sound of voices, the old shaman's eyes flickered open. Looking surprised by the ring of faces surrounding him, he turned to Doña Luisa. "Maria, *mi esposa*, have you come to take me with you? I am ready to go."

Julio's eyes widened. Maria was the name of Don Rodrigo's wife, who had died twenty years ago.

"No...no, *Abuelo*," Josefina said. "Your wife is not here. That's..."

Doña Luisa grabbed her arm. "No," she said. "*No, le molestes.* Do not upset him." She tried to shake off the alarm we all felt.

"Here, Carrie. You boil some water. I will crush the cowfoot leaves. We must make the tea to stop the bleeding."

Don Rodrigo reached out with his right hand. "*Agua, por favor.*" His voice was a whisper. After he managed to drink a dipperful, his eyes closed again, and he drifted away.

Doña Luisa gave us orders. "Josefina, you wash the blood and the mud off his arm. And Julio, when the tea is ready, you bathe his head with it, but do it very softly. Later, when it is cool enough, we will give him some to drink."

Twenty Three

Hours crept by as Julio and I kept a vigil, searching Don Rodrigo's face for signs of consciousness. Josefina, too, did her part, keeping the children as quiet as she could. As the sun faded, we lit candles. Doña Luisa sat by the bed, working her rosary beads before calling on the Mayan spirits for help. Julio strung himself a hammock in the other room, and I laid down on the floor, nearby, and slept.

At daybreak, Don Rodrigo opened his eyes, calling out. "Where is my Maria, *mi esposa*? She was just here. I saw her."

Doña Luisa lifted her head from the armchair where she'd dozed, and Josefina came to the bedside. "No, *Papa. Lo siento.* I'm sorry. You were dreaming."

Watching a tear trickle down his cheek, I realized that I'd never seen Don Rodrigo cry before Then he turned to Doña Luisa, "*Agua, agua,*" he croaked through parched lips.

Gently, I lifted his head from the pillow so that Doña Luisa could hold the cup to his lips. He drank greedily, leaning forward to drain the last drops, until with a cry, he fell back onto the pillow. It was then that I saw the discolored mass protruding from the top of his upper arm.

"He must have dislocated his shoulder in the fall," I said. "No wonder he is in such pain. How did we not see it?"

Don Rodrigo looked around with a puzzled expression, his gaze moving from Doñã Luisa to Julio to me to Josefina. "*Por qué están todos aquí?* Why are you here?" he asked, sounding annoyed.

"Why are we here? You scared us. You fell on the path. You dislocated your shoulder. We were afraid," I said. "That's why we're here."

He accepted my answer and dozed off again. When he awoke, we spooned ginger tea and water into his mouth. Doña Luisa bathed his bruised and swollen arm several times, taking care not to move it. At even the slightest touch, he cried, "Stop, stop!"

Even though the dried blood had been washed from his temple, his arm, resting above the blanket, was still an odd shade of purple.

Soon, Doña Luisa was ready to turn her attention to the dislocated shoulder. "I must fix it now. The longer we wait," she said, "the worse it will become."

"Is there anything I can do to help?" I asked.

"The pain will be bad. Find him something to bite down on."

Don Rodrigo snorted at the insult in her words. When I offered a clean towel to put between his teeth, he brushed my hand away. "*No quiero*, I don't want that; bring me the rum." Julio found a half-full bottle and brought it to the patient's lips. Once the old man drank deep, he signaled he was ready. Massaging the arm for several minutes, Doña Luisa first gently, then firmly pushed the shoulder back in place. He cried out in pain. Even though I'd never heard such a bellow pass his lips. Doña Luisa looked satisfied with the result. "The worst is over," she said. Sweating profusely in the heat of the small house, she quickly went outside to cool off. No one would have blamed her for wanting to escape for a few minutes.

To the patient's displeasure, Julio moved the bottle out of reach. "Stop. Leave it right there where I can see it," the old man directed. "And give it to me when I ask for it, pronto" He held out his good hand, motioning for the rum. After another gulp, he sat back to rest. I swallowed a smile as Julio, and I exchanged knowing looks. Perhaps, some of the pain was subsiding and our patient was feeling stronger.

Doña Luisa came back in. "How do you feel, my friend?" she asked.

"*Tengo hambre.* I'm hungry. I want to eat."

The chickens on the farm, valued for their eggs, were almost like family, but when Doña Luisa suggested that Don Rodrigo would benefit from a hearty broth, Josefina picked up a hatchet and went outside. Soon we heard a squawk, followed by sad cries from the children. The unlucky bird, butchered and dressed, found its way into the soup pot and soon, the smell of the simmering stock filled the small house.

As Josefina brought in the bowl of soup, the old man sat up taller. Aside from a couple of spoonsful of rice and beans, I remembered that none of us had eaten in many hours and the smell of her cooking was tantalizing. Once Don Rodrigo was served, Josefina called in the children. She set out bowls of caldo, a stew of root vegetables, corn and chicken on the table next to her homemade tortillas. After the children were fed, Doña Luisa, Julio, and I each managed to grab a bowlful of the satisfying Mayan meal, gratefully sopping up any remaining broth.

"*Josefina, eres una buena cocinera,*" Doña Luisa said.

"*Gracias,*" Josefina said. Her curt reply barely acknowledging the compliment as her due.

Once the shoulder was back in the socket, Doña Luisa came

daily to massage and knead the swollen arm. The fourth day, she nodded and smiled. Much of the swelling was down. She was ready for the next step. She motioned to Julio, "I need some cloth for the sling," she said.

Julio looked to Josefina. Without a word, she went outside to the clothesline and pulled a sheet from the line, twisting the edges, pulling it with her muscled brown arms until it ripped. She tore again and halved the piece of fabric. Then she folded the clean white cloth into a triangle, handing it to Doña Luisa.

Julio propped his uncle up in bed. When the sling was ready, Doña Luisa carefully lifted the injured arm. "Slowly, slowly," the patient warned, his eyes full of fire.

"Don't worry, I know what to do. I have set many bones in my time." Cradling the elbow, she gently pulled both ends of cloth around his neck, tying them together. Finally, with the sling in place, she asked, "How does it feel now?"

"It hurts, *Mamacita*, but I think I will live. I've suffered worse. Julio, more rum."

Outside, there was the sound of tires on gravel. I hoped it wasn't a patient coming for treatment. The children ran in shouting, "*Gringos, gringos aquí.*"

All eyes turned in my direction and as the resident gringa, it felt like my job to check the source of their excitement. Outside were two familiar-looking Americans standing next to the vehicle. Though I remembered their names, they re-introduced themselves. It was the two scientists I'd met at the healers' conference.

Brad McNally stepped forward. He was a thirty-something American wearing a baseball hat, and a New York Yankees t-shirt. His colleague, Debra Cook, was a pale young woman in Bermuda shorts and a wide-brimmed straw hat. Smiling broadly, she extended her hand. "Carrie Mullen, you have a way of turning up, don't you? This is great."

"We didn't expect to see you here," Brad said. "We were in the audience when Don Rodrigo was recognized for all his work. But we didn't get a chance to talk to him that day because he left early. When someone told us where we might find him, we decided to come looking."

"Everyone we've talked to since the conference said that he is one of the most knowledgeable of all the healers of Belize," Debra said. "He's a legend."

"Yes, that's true. He's all of that and more. Usually, he'd be happy to talk to you, but I'm sorry to tell you this is not a good time. He suffered an accident."

"Should we go for help? Is there anything we can do?"

"No, he's well cared for, and I'm happy to say he seems to be doing better."

"Thank goodness for that. Any chance you might have a few minutes to talk now? I know it's not a good time, but we've come a long way." He went to the trunk of the car, digging around in a bag until he pulled out a sheet of paper. "We wanted to ask you about this."

My eyes popped. There was my signature scrawled at the bottom of a letter. It was one I'd written many months ago. "Where did you get that?" I asked.

"One of the scientists we're working with at the NIH had it in his file in Washington. When we got the contract to come to Belize to do research, he suggested that we try to get in touch with you."

I had almost forgotten my early efforts to communicate with fellow scientists. Now I was reminded of my earlier dreams of establishing research links to the outside world. During my first year, I had sent both hard copies and emails to a variety of government entities and scientific foundations to try to connect. I did get a few return emails, thanking me for my efforts to communicate. One botanical society referred me to another botanist who was working in Brazil. Off the grid, it became more difficult to keep up communication. Little by little, my efforts fell away as I came to accept the fact that the scientific community was not ready to acknowledge the traditional healers of Belize.

"Our colleague, Dr. Minton, did send a reply to you over a year ago. Did you get it?"

I shook my head. "It doesn't ring a bell. Add to that, some earlier problems with internet connections here."

"Unfortunately, I guess he didn't realize that even getting email in Belize can be challenging. Anyway, we're in luck. Another colleague, Jeff Donnelly mentioned you too. We found you and you are part of the reason we're here. You see, you're famous."

I laughed then, but with mixed emotion. After failed efforts in setting up the lab with Mel, my disappointment in Jeff, and the threats symbolized by someone like Roz, hope was fading.

So many times, I annoyed Don Rodrigo with my thousands of questions, but he was still more than willing to share his knowledge. And I was grateful for all the time we spent, digging our way through the jungle, chopping roots, gathering vines, and collecting leaves. I still had all the notes I'd taken during the days, weeks, and months spent with my teacher. I'd recorded names of the plants, where to find them, how to prepare them and, even how they each worked Best of all, when I watched him as he treated his patients with the plants we'd gathered, I was able to see the healing results with my own eyes. Now that viable collaborators from the outside world were here, I wondered if it was too little, too late.

"You said you had a contract to do research? Do you work for the NIH?" I asked.

"No, we're free-lance contractors. Belize has so few scientists to call their own, they hired us to gather the information. We have a six-month time frame to do our research. Did I mention that we're staying at the Rio Blanco Hotel in San Ignacio?" Debra said.

"I don't think so," I said.

"Well, anyway, we've found you now. Do you want to work with us?" Debra asked.

Was it possible that the outside world might still find a use for the knowledge and wisdom of the plants and the healers like Don Rodrigo?

What should I do?

"Yes," I said.

Twenty Four

Doña Luisa left her house in the village at dawn, walking for two miles until she reached the narrow foot bridge that crossed over the river. After that she would follow the well-worn forest path to the farm, all to spend the day caring for Don Rodrigo.

"Is it difficult for you to spend so much time here?" I asked. I knew her husband had died years earlier, but she still spoke often of her children and I thought perhaps, like so many Mayan families, they all lived together.

"*Mi casa esta vacia.* My house is empty. My children moved to Belize City." There was sadness in her voice.

"But don't you have your own patients who come to you for treatment?"

"Yes, but now is a slow time for me. Not many babies are ready to be born this month. I am on vacation." She laughed.

"More like a working vacation," I said.

"Last night I had a dream," she said, her expression turning serious. "The spirits told me he will heal but it must be done slowly. They told me it is my duty to help, to be here."

Maybe the spirits were right. When I worried that Don Rodrigo was still in bed. Doña Luisa said "Let him stay there until he is ready to get up. His body is tired, but his spirit is bright. When he is ready, he will walk."

Even when the healer, himself, was in a state of recovery, some things didn't change. The flow of those ailing and in need of treatment continued to arrive at his door. Patients from the village and beyond still came in search of treatment. And Doña Luisa was ready to help. Perhaps, I expected a certain amount of professional rivalry between the two Mayan healers, but, to my surprise, the old man was more than willing for his friend to step in. He encouraged her to treat everyone who came to the door, telling her to accept any payment they offered.

Happily, Doña Luisa wanted to do all she could. As the village midwife, she was skilled in the use of herbs and plants. She told stories of the snakebites she had treated and the many bones she had set. Still, if there were questions about a diagnosis, she and Don Rodrigo would confer and then she would follow through with the treatment they agreed on. As the days passed, it seemed that they conferred less, and she treated more. To my surprise, the old shaman accepted this willingly. "*Ella es mi companera*, she is my partner."

On my next visit, I noticed she was wearing a fresh white dress with colorful embroidery around the neckline. Her shining black hair was freshly washed. "Doña Luisa, you look lovely. *Muy linda*." She'd blossomed in this new setting, needing only to be given the acknowledgement of her expertise.

Witnessing this harmony, I tried hard to ignore a pang of jealousy that shot across my chest. Didn't I also have knowledge gleaned from the many months spent at my teacher's side? In my heart, I once believed all I needed was the chance to use my hard-earned skills. Sadly, now I saw that Doña Luisa had something that I would never have. It was one thing to be the healer's assistant as I had been. It was another thing to be the healer.

If villagers came for treatment, and Doña Luisa wasn't there, I offered my help. Even though Don Rodrigo complemented me on my knowledge and encouraged patients to speak to me of their concerns, I saw a reluctance in their eyes. I realized that I could never elicit the trust they gave to one of their own. And Doña Luisa had their trust, she was of their heritage, accepted in a way that I never would be.

Some days later, battered arm in the sling, Don Rodrigo was ready to get out of bed. He called for Julio to help him up. "I am tired of looking at these ugly walls. I want to feel the sun on my face." He pointed to the open door.

Ensconced on the small porch, he was content just to breath the air and watch Josefina's grandchildren chase the chickens around the yard. "*Qué hermoso es el mundo.* How beautiful is the world we live in."

One day, when Doña Luisa was busy elsewhere, Don Rodrigo motioned me to him. "Sit, *mi hija*, sit," he said. "I want to tell you something." Leaning close, he whispered in my ear. "I want Dona Luisa to come and live on the farm. I know you will say I am too old. And yes, it is true, I am old. But I have been lonely since my Maria died. Once I get better, you'll see. I still know how to keep a woman warm in my bed."

"Does she know this?" I tried to keep the surprise out of my voice. "Did you ask her?"

"*Si, si, si*! Yes, and she too, is lonely. We have known each other for many years. She knew my Maria. They were friends. And many years ago, I worked with her husband in the camps until he died. She is much younger, but she still thinks I am handsome, *muy guapo.*"

"Yes, I think so, too. You are very handsome."

He smiled. "Now our friendship can become something more.

She was willing to stay but she worries that with Josefina and the children, there will be no room for her."

Don Rodrigo didn't want this to get in the way of his newfound happiness. The next step, he said was for Julio to build a separate cabin so they would have some privacy.

He called his nephew to him. As he explained his plan, a puzzled frown crossed Julio's face.

"You want a new house?" Julio asked.

"Just a little cabin for Doña Luisa so she will be happy. Will you do this for me? Will you build this for me?"

"Yes, of course. I am happy to do this if it will make you feel better. But we have no money to pay for it. You know the Mennonites want to be paid in cash for their lumber."

"Don't worry. I will find a way," Don Rodrigo said.

It was growing dark. I asked Julio to drive me back to the lodge. As he went out to start the car, Don Rodrigo whispered. "Where is the money?"

"It's where you told me to put it. In the safe at the Seven Sisters Lodge."

"Carrie, *mi hija*, I want you to bring me some of it. Just bring half, not all of it. It should be just enough for Julio to buy the lumber from the Mennonites, so he can build something for my Luisa. I want her to stay here. Don't tell him where the money came from. It's better if he doesn't know."

Julio and I had worked hard together when he helped me set up the lab. I'd seen his skills. He was more than capable of doing a good job on the construction if he had the tools at hand.

Excited by my errand, I went back to the lodge. James was off at an environmental meeting, but I found Gloria in the lobby. "Do you remember the bag of money I gave you for safe-keeping?"

"Of course. Don Rodrigo's savings? No worries. It's still locked up in our office safe, right where we left it."

I nodded, sighing inwardly with relief.

"Shall we go get it now?"

"Yes," I said, "if you have time."

From the office safe we extracted the healer's life savings, so patiently collected over the years. When he gave me the money, I remembered Don Rodrigo telling me that he knew how much money he had saved. He'd never said how much was there, and I hadn't counted it when he gave it to me for safe keeping. There wasn't time then. Now, back in my room, I spread the contents of the bag out on my bed.

I was moved at the sight of the small collection of folded bills tightly rubber-banded together. The frayed elastic, diminished by age, snapped apart in my hands. In the fragile bundles there were Belizean dollars, American dollars, even a few quetzales, the currency of Guatemala. I shook my head in amazement at the sight of old, wrinkled British five-pound notes left over from the days when Belize was a British colony years ago. I gathered the American dollars together, put the rest of the money back in the bag and went to look for Gloria.

The current exchange rate was two Belize dollars for one American dollar. Together Gloria and I counted out four hundred dollars in American currency which she was more than happy to transform into eight hundred Belize dollars. I looked forward to delivering the cash to Don Rodrigo. Then Julio could purchase the lumber and roofing materials needed to make Don Rodrigo's dream a reality. Gloria and I returned the rest of the money back into the safe at the lodge office and I tucked the ready cash into a hiding place in a shoe box in my closet, ready to be deliver it the next day. It would be a good start.

With Don Rodrigo on the mend, I felt safe enough to take some time away from his bedside. How many weeks had passed since the day my teacher visited the lab to give his blessing? Ronnie was there that day and the two had connected. It was there that the idea for the ayahuasca retreat took shape. How was Ronnie doing? And what about the ayahuasca project?

My thoughts turned back to the little lab sitting lonely and unused in the midst of Mel's compound. All the equipment was there. The microscopes, the plant presses, the dehydration system. Test tubes, petri dishes and other paraphernalia were all in place and ready and waiting for experiments that never materialized.

I was pleased when Brad and Debra reached out to me, asking for an update on what I'd been doing recently. I appreciated the positive connection and my professional pride made me want to impress these visitors. We all valued scientific research and I was anxious to talk shop with them.

I invited them to meet me at the lodge for lunch. "My treat," I said. "I'll meet you outside near the front steps to the lobby." Once they arrived, we made a quick tour of the grounds and Debra's eyes grew large as she took in the blooming orchids, the bright colors of the bird-of-paradise plants and the lush greenery.

We found a table outdoors on the veranda. "Lucky you," Debra said. "It feels like I'm sitting in the middle of a travel magazine."

"Yes, this beats hell out of our hotel in San Ignacio." Brad added. "How did you manage to get here?"

"I'd been staying at Don Rodrigo's farm and you saw how small it is. I moved here as a temporary measure. Soon after, I got some work with an American entrepreneur and that helped me to pay the rent here. Perhaps, you've heard of him. Mel Powers?"

"The name's familiar. I heard him mentioned somewhere," Brad said.

I tried to read the expression in his eyes.

"What's he doing here in this out-of-the-way corner of Belize?" Debra asked.

"There have been multiple stories," I said. "My guess is that he's laying low but if and when you meet him, he'll probably come up with his own version of events for you. Maybe we could take a field trip out to his compound if you are up for it."

The Washington researchers were interested. "We'd love to see the lab. How is today?" Brad wondered.

Debra had already asked me to consider helping them. From what I could tell, they seemed to be working out of their car and their deadline loomed ahead. A thought occurred. Maybe Mel would consider renting the space to them.

"Let me give him a heads-up and I'll get right back to you." I called Mel's cell and got his message. Then I texted. He was out of town he said but gave the go-ahead. Ronnie would be at the gate to let us in.

Twenty Five

Debra and Brad kept telling me how anxious they were to see what they called my "jungle lab". When Mel wouldn't be around, but we were still welcome to visit. Just as well, I thought, we'll be able to wander about on our own.

Debra took the wheel, and we were on our way. At the sight of the closed gate, Brad's eyebrows shot up. "Looks like our host, Mel is pretty serious about his security," he said. He leaned across, "Debra, give them a toot."

I stuck my head out of the rear passenger window. "Ronnie, it's me, Carrie." The gate came up. As we parked, Ronnie sauntered over, looking cheerful. His even disposition was a relaxing change from the once-jittery guard whose fears could erupt at the sound of a car backfiring.

"Ronnie, say hello to Debra and Brad. They're here from D.C. and I wanted to show them the lab," I said.

"Hi, guys," he said. "Welcome to Belize."

"Everything OK on this end?" I asked.

"It's always quiet when the boss is away." He wiped pretend sweat from his brow. "He and Gabrielle took a few days off. Think they went to the beach."

"Enjoy your down time."

"For sure, I will. And here's some good news." He gave my arm a friendly squeeze. "From now on you can call me "*el jefe*." I'm the new security chief. Armand, the head guard, quit and my promotion kicked in last week. We also hired a new guy, Carlos. He knows Julio, by the way."

I waved "hello" to the new recruit at the guard station door. "I've been seeing a lot of Julio. He's been taking me out to see his uncle."

"How is the old guy?" Ronnie said. "I heard that he wasn't doing well. I've been meaning to go over and check on him."

"You heard right. He's the reason I've been scarce. He was in bad shape after a serious fall. Thankfully, he seems to be on the mend. Best of all, he has a new partner, Doña Luisa"

Ronnie's face lit up. "New partner, how?'

"Girlfriend, life partner, amiga. Take your pick. All I know is that both of them are very content. You can imagine how he's perking up. She'll even be coming to live with him at the farm. Julio is even building her a little house."

"Awesome! When Mel gets back, I'll go over to check up on him. He's my man!"

"You know he loves company."

Giving a playful salute, I asked, "Considering your new title, do we have your permission to take a stroll around and check out the lab?"

"Go for it," he said.

While Ronnie and I gabbed, Brad and Debra craned their necks, taking in Mel's compound. I knew they were anxious to see it all. Given the chance later, I'd circle back to catch up with Ronnie and see if anything interesting might have happened recently.

Looking around it felt like forever since I'd been there, but maybe no more than a couple of weeks. At that time, Laura, the Miami Herald reporter came to interview Mel. So far, Mel's hope of generating press on his new project had not born fruit. To date, there had been no mention of Mel or his plans for the ayahuasca retreat in the Florida press. Still, the reporter hadn't forgotten Belize. She'd done a major story on the destruction of the rainforests of Central and South America and the conflict of the indigenous people guarding against the poachers, and loggers seeking to rob the forest of its treasures, destroying it in the process. When she sent me the article, *Forest Guardians Do Battle Against Invaders,* I was gratified to see that she'd given Belize a couple of paragraphs. James was thrilled that she'd quoted him, too. I planned to keep in touch, sending updates when I could.

My thoughts were sidetracked as Brad took off, pointing excitedly at a pair of red and black macaws flying overhead. "Wow! Look at that." He sprinted away in their direction.

"He's an avid birder," Debra said.

"He's come to the perfect spot for that," I said.

It was impossible not to follow the birds as they glided toward the river. Brad took out his phone to catch a photo, but the pair perched for only a moment before flitting away. The water's edge, teeming with life, drew us in. Debra pointed to a small crocodile slithering through the muddy, slow-moving water. "At first, I thought it was a floating log. Is that what they call the Morelet croc?" she asked.

Before I could answer, the reptile in question climbed onto the bank, lunging at a tree frog perched on a low stump. Too late, the frog jumped at the predator's approach. Sadly, we watched its legs disappear into the larger reptile's vise-like jaws.

"Such is life in the jungle." Debra murmured as we turned back toward the compound.

After that excitement, it was time for the guided tour. "Follow me," I said.

The visitors were full of questions. "I'm dying to hear about Mel and how he came to Belize." Brad said.

"There's plenty to tell," I laughed. And I had many a story I could have shared. Instead, I chose a laundered version of events, spinning a tale of the American tech millionaire searching for spiritual enlightenment in nature. Today, they seemed to buy it, but later, they might come to know another version of the story.

Next stop was the freshly built gazebo, the scene of our recent tea ceremony. Looking around, Brad asked, "Were you a participant, an observer or a guide in the ayahuasca ceremony?"

"A participant. Our goal was to help Ronnie with his PTSD. He was anxious to try it, but he didn't want to go it alone. So, it was the three of us, Mel, Ronnie and me."

"Was it your first experience?"

"No, I'd tried it once before. It was the first year I was studying with Don Rodrigo. From what I've seen, it has value as a therapeutic tool. I can see that now in Ronnie. For people who've suffered trauma, the healing can be very real."

"It's becoming quite a thing in the States," Debra said. "I wonder though about some of the so-called ceremony leaders. These days, anyone can call themselves a shaman and far too many do. And what are their credentials?"

"For sure, nobody is handing out a certificate." Brad said.

"We don't have that problem here. Don Rodrigo is a true shaman, an experienced healer. With him present, we all felt safe. Still the physical challenges of the ceremony are real. To be honest, I'm thinking that the two times I participated might have been more than enough for me." They laughed.

As the sun climbed higher in the sky, the heat bore down through the trees. Debra was fanning herself. "How long does it take to get used to this heat?"

"Let me get you something cool to drink," I said. We headed to the main house and I used my key to unlock the front door. Brad and Debra stayed outside on the veranda, but they couldn't resist peeking through the open front door. Even though the interior was a bit of a mess, Debra still looked impressed by the tropical comfort of the place.

Custom-made beige sofas sat atop black slate floors. Around the room, several large pieces of pre-Columbian art added an unexpected touch of luxury to a house sitting in the middle of the rainforest. Pointing to a tall mahogany sculpture, Brad gave a low whistle, "Not bad."

Refreshed by the cool water, we were ready for the main event. I'd saved the best for last and they were anxious to see the lab. My heart skipped a beat when I found the door unlocked. Thankfully, it was just as I'd left it, the pristine equipment still safely in place.

Debra's eyes lit up. "Pretty impressive for something that's sitting here in the middle of the jungle. I wasn't expecting this."

"I have to give Mel credit," I said. "He was not stingy. When I was ordering the equipment and supplies, he told me to get the best. Once everything was installed, we never really got a chance to use it. There was research I hoped to work on, plant samples I wanted to test but Mel's agenda was always changing. He wanted the big payoff and he wanted it fast."

"What do you mean, payoff?" Brad asked.

"Somehow, Mel actually managed to obtain a grant from the Belize government. The initial plan he laid out was for us to identify a new plant-based antibiotic. His idea was that a product would be produced here, providing a way to create jobs for the local people. But we never made any progress with that. Before we got started, Mel's hyper personality went into overdrive. He has a way of jumping from one thing to another."

Debra was only listening with half an ear. "Um-hm," she said while she ran her hand appreciatively over the smooth counter surface. And Brad looked longingly toward the back wall where the electrical equipment was mounted.

"Mel met another entrepreneur, a pharmaceutical executive. She was as hardnosed as he was. Initially there was a discussion of a plant cure for diabetes. I tried to steer her to one of the most widely used plants in Belize, a vine called *sorosi*."

"I've read articles about it," Debra said.

"You've probably seen it along the roadside, climbing over fences. Sorosi grows wild almost everywhere," I said. "It cleans the blood, and many believe that the tea possesses agents that fight against diseases related to diabetes,"

"Yes, we also considered taking a look at that." Brad said. "From what I hear, so are some big drug firms."

"Recently I heard there were some negative research findings," Debra said. "Especially when children ingested the fruits of the plant."

"Yes, I know. That's a roadblock. It was tested and approved for external use only. So that idea was put on hold. When they talked about ayahuasca as the remedy for PTSD, Mel shared the positive results Ronnie experienced. Soon, the two of them were talking about producing it in capsule form. They discussed growing the plants on nearby acreage Mel bought. There was even talk of trying to set up clinical trials. It blew my mind."

"Clinical trials in the middle of the jungle?" Brad laughed. "That would be tough going."

"Yes, I guess Roz, the pharma executive, finally woke up to that fact. Soon after, she lost interest in Belize. The last I heard she was on her way to Brazil, on the trail of another indigenous shaman. But enough history. Tell me about your research goals," I said.

"We've been tasked with identifying the top one hundred medicinal plant species in Belize, species that produce identifiable results," Brad said.

"So, we were given six months to identify and gather active plant species to send back to the NIH. Since we've already been here a couple months, we're going to need a lot of help. We don't have a lot of time," Debra said. "Our contract calls for us to deliver a product three months after we get back."

"We knew we'd be able to collect the plants but there was some concern about how we'd be able to prepare samples. That was before we saw the sweet set-up you have here. If we're going follow the NIH protocols for shipping," Brad said. "We need a drying oven or a freeze dryer."

"As you can see, we have both," I said. Pointing to the oven and the freezer in place on the back wall of the lab, hooked up and ready to go.

"I didn't bring the submission guidelines with me," Brad said. "But I'm thinking that what we need to do with the plant samples can be done here. You can dry the plant material either in the dryer or freeze dry it, right?"

"No problem," I said.

"Once the dried material is pulverized to a consistent particle size, the samples will be weighed into capsules for analysis. Looks like you have everything we need to do that," Debra said. "Any chance we might persuade Mel to let us do the work here?"

Twenty Six

Just back from a beach getaway on the Caribbean, Gabrielle was excited to tell me about a property for sale. "It's a small hotel with a bar and restaurant on the water at San Pedro. It needs a few month's work, but it could be ready for tourists by next season," Gabrielle said. "Mel might make an offer."

When she flashed photos of a cloudless sky, white sand, and blue water I could see the attraction. "It looks like a beautiful vacation spot," I said. "Is that why you went there?" I asked.

"Not really. We went to the coast so Mel could meet with one of his lawyers at the airport. But he just happened to hear about this hotel for sale and we took a look. He thinks the price is right but, first, he's gonna check his finances."

"Fingers crossed, I hope it works out," I said. *Why rain on her parade.*

Though the additional income wouldn't be much, I suggested to Gabrielle that Mel could grab some fast cash by renting the lab. She agreed to whisper the idea in his ear.

Even before I introduced Mel to Debra and Brad, Gabrielle told me she'd put a bug in Mel's ear. She thought he liked the idea so when Brad came with cash in hand, offering to pay three months up front, Mel liked the idea even better.

"You three have some connections in common," I said, watching them shake on the deal. "These two have been keeping the Belize Department of Economic Development posted on their progress."

Mel's eyes lit up. "In that case I'll rent the lab to you for the next three months and I'll throw in an extra month free. Just make sure the Belize government knows we're working together. Who knows, maybe we can even find a way to hire a couple of local people. I want the Belize government to know I'm doing my part," Mel said.

Was it a wake-up call? I hadn't heard him mention anything about the six-figure government grant he'd received months ago. So far, not one of the promised local jobs had materialized.

Even though the NIH scientists now had a lab at their disposal, they felt the pressure building. Filled with a growing concern about the project deadline, Brad and Debra were getting nervous, looking for any help they could find. They were under a deadline to produce what they called the project deliverables. When I asked for specifics, Debra described a database and plant samples to be processed and sent to several labs in the States.

"How many species do you need to identify for your NIH contract?" I asked.

"For the initial six months, we're tasked with identifying two hundred plants and providing extensive information on one hundred. Then after the first series, there could be more," Debra said.

"We were able to buy samples from some of the healers we met at the conference," Brad said. "There was an herbalist from

Belize City, and we got fifty different samples from her."

You didn't mention that before.

"We're looking for any help we can get. In San Ignacio, I've been hearing about Galen University. Carrie, what do you know about the school?" Brad asked.

Galen University, on the edge of San Ignacio, is one of the few institutions of higher learning in the country. It's about twenty miles north of Mel's compound. "I only visited Galen once. That was when Mel gave a presentation to their board on his vision of "entrepreneurial spirit." While we were there, I remember the university president saying that the school was founded in hopes that it would attract students and economic activity to this corner of the country."

Even though the small university could not compare with anything back in the States, the two scientists made an appointment to visit the campus. "Carrie, do you want to come with us."

"Sure." Curious to see what Galen's lab looked like, I was happy to tag along. Since meeting with Brad and Debra, I'd come to value a connection with the scientific community. And I was grateful for these new colleagues.

"It's worth the time it would take for us to check the school," Debra said. "Maybe we can get some help from them. If we can hire a couple of science instructors who teach the lab courses, they'd already have some experience with lab work. We wouldn't have to train them beyond showing them how to use the drying equipment."

The science department chairman was cordial and happy to give the Washington visitors a tour. Showing off the university science lab, he described his hopes for expansion but, presently there was only the one lab and it got heavy use from the basic biology and chemistry students. While there were plans to upgrade the facilities, that time had not yet come. Unfortunately, their full schedule meant that the school would be unable to free up any time for additional use. We thanked him and left.

In the car, I couldn't help saying, "Their lab is a lot more spacious, but I wouldn't call it up to standards."

"Yes, your lab is smaller, but it's makes up for it by having the latest equipment."

Even if their lab space wasn't available, Debra wondered if there might be another way for Galen and the NIH to work together. "I should have asked the department head if we could get a couple of faculty to give us some hours every week. I think that would be a help," she said.

"Something to think about," Brad said. "But how have we been so oblivious to what we have right in front of us? Not only do we have the lab, but here's the person who knows it best right under our noses." His eyes caught mine in the rearview mirror. "What do you say, Carrie, do you want to participate in the project? Unfortunately, your name won't be on the documentation, but, at least, we'll be able to provide a good hourly rate. We do have a budget."

Hmm, I wondered. If Mel was struggling, maybe this would help me pay the rent.

"Are you in?"

"Of course, I'm in. Debra already asked me a while back. I thought it was a done deal. Don't you guys talk to each other?"

"I'm sorry," Debra said. "I guess I figured it went without saying."

"Debra can be absent-minded," Brad said A look passed between them.

And now that you bring up a budget, it occurs to me that I have something that will save you guys a huge amount of time. I've already compiled a database of well over one hundred of the most widely used medicinal plants in this part of the country? Did I mention it?"

"No, you sure didn't. Can we look?" Debra asked.

"I'm still tweaking the final version. I've been working on it almost since the day I arrived three years ago."

"That's a long time," Brad said.

"But it should be ready in a couple of days."

"Dad, I need your advice. I really got myself into it. You know all the plant descriptions and content I've been collecting since I got here?"

"Sure. How's that going?"

"Well, I've got all the raw data in my notebooks. I'm using it to create a spreadsheet and a database. That's the good news. Since the last time we talked, I've made a connection with two scientists working with NIH."

"Awesome. Sounds like things are coming together."

"You know I've spent thousands of hours on this. If I can get it into a useful package, I think it will be valuable to them. But I don't think I should just hand it over, do you?"

"Are you kidding? Of course not. That's your hard work. And they should pay for it," Dad said. "You've earned this with sweat equity. It's the NIH, kiddo. I'm sure they can afford it. Promise me you won't give it away!"

"But how should I do it? What price tag should I put on it?"

"I can't tell you that, honey. But here's a piece of advice," he laughed. "Just pretend you're Mel!"

"Thanks, Dad. Good idea." I laughed. "You are the best."

Now it was my turn to be nervous. I'd made a claim about my plant database and now I'd have to make good on it. There were valuable records listing several hundred plants and the ways that Don Rodrigo and other local healers used them. When I'd spread all the paperwork out in my room, the notes covered the bed, the dresser and even the floor. Unfortunately, some of the plant samples were crumpled beyond redemption, but there still might be time to collect more.

When I came to live at the farm, I brought a laptop with me, expecting to use it every day. If it was a quiet afternoon at the farm, I'd hoped to take my notebook out and sit on the porch, balancing it on my knees while I scribbled away. Once the notes were ready, I expected to transfer them to my computer, creating a database. Too bad my time in the field hadn't gone according to plan.

I remembered when Don Rodrigo laughingly called my computer the "magic box. "*Mi hija,* do you think it will do its magic *aqui?*" he asked.

Sadly, he was right. Off the grid, as we were, there was no electricity, no way to charge a dead computer battery, and often, no internet signal. If I was desperate, I could go into the village and charge my laptop battery at the grocery store, but that was iffy. Many times, their generator was running low. Or it might be out of commission altogether.

Technology, the magic of the modern world, didn't always work out so well in the bush. While I was living on the farm, I kept my records the only way I could, filling hundreds of notebook pages by hand. It seemed impossible, in that jungle setting, to complete the work then. But now it was imperative.

Why did you wait? I asked myself. *Why didn't you start putting it in the computer sooner?* It was a hard question to answer. Was it because I believed that I should commit the knowledge to memory? Had I believed that, like my teacher, I should know all the names and uses of the plants by heart? Part of me said yes. Still, I should have known that I couldn't have it both ways. Though it was my dream, I wasn't a healer like Don

Rodrigo. And until that day came, if it ever did, I was a scientist.

I scanned everything in front of me. For each plant, there was a format: I planned to identify each plant and categorize how it was used by the traditional healers as they treated different ailments. Should the plant material be ground into a powder or boiled into a tea to be drunk? Was a substance to be taken internally or applied externally, made into a salve to soothe skin rashes? All these methods needed to be classified and labeled.

I thought of copal, one of the most used plant remedies. It was valued for its many curative properties. Its powdered bark was applied to wounds and used to treat infections, while the bark boiled into a tea helped with stomach ailments, expelling intestinal parasites. The copal resin was even used to treat painful dental cavities. In my notes I'd listed all the variations, to be sure. Other herbs, like sorosi, were used to treat a variety of different ailments. It was the same with widely used plants like wild coca, baby's tears, vervain, and contribo.

But now my challenge was to transfer everything to the usable computer database I claimed to have. And so, for the next week, I spent my nights working well past midnight to transform raw pages of notes into a useful tool that would meet at least a basic level of scientific protocol.

"Our NIH contract also calls for us to interview as many traditional healers as we can identify. That hasn't been easy and we're way behind on that," Brad said. "I don't have to tell you most of them are in remote areas. Some don't speak English. Debra's Spanish is fairly good, but we don't know the Mayan tongue. I have to admit that when we first got here, we didn't get off to the best start. We came on too strong and didn't take time for the people to feel comfortable with us."

"Our cultural sensitivity training was sadly lacking," Debra admitted with a rueful smile. "After we stuck cameras and microphones in their faces, more than a few of the healers we talked to told us they were not interested in sharing their knowledge with us. I guess I couldn't blame them." She smiled sadly. "We learned the hard way."

"But it would really help, if we could get some information from Don Rodrigo to add to our report," Brad said. "We interviewed several healers at the conference where we first met you, but your teacher is so well known, it would be a privilege to include him in the group. Do you think he might meet with us?"

Now that I was a bona fide member of the team, I offered to try to make that happen. Even more important, it would be a good excuse to visit the farm. I called Julio. "Things are quiet," he said. "Now would be a good time to come. Some company would lift my uncle's spirits."

It was only a ten-minute drive and I was anxious to see Don Rodrigo. Debra, Brad and I piled into their SUV. Just before we pulled out of the gate, Ronnie appeared, a case of the local Beliken beer under his arm. "I have a present for the old man," he said with a grin. "Can I tag along? It's my day off."

We found him sitting with Doña Luisa on his porch. His smile was proof that his spirits had returned, and I hoped he would be pleased to have new people to listen to his stories. With the help of a cane, he rose from his chair to greet us.

Introducing Debra and Brad to Don Rodrigo brought back times when he welcomed other foreign scientists to his farm. "With your permission, we would like to take samples from the plants growing nearby in the forest," Brad said.

"I cannot take you to them, as I have done in the past. But Doña Luisa and Carrie know where to find the plants. And I will help you if I can."

While the two Americans spoke with my teacher, I went in search of Julio. Walking past the vegetable garden, I could see the results of his labor. The small cabin was already under roof and there were frames for the doors and windows. I stuck my head inside. "Julio, where are you?"

"I'm outside."

I found him resting under a tree. "What's wrong?" His expression had a downward turn. "You don't look happy."

He gestured at the house. "It was coming along but now I've worked through all the lumber," he said. "*Necessito mas dinero.* I need money for the dry wall and money for the floor. Don Rodrigo even promised his lady a bathtub."

"Wow, a bathtub? I bet the neighbors would come to see that," I said. Memories of the metal tub I'd bathed in flashed through my mind.

'You're right. It would be an attraction."

"But how would you be able to get water for the tub?"

"I came up with an idea to catch the rainwater and pipe it inside. Pretty cool, hunh?"

"Very cool. Julio, you amaze me."

"The tub idea really has Josefina pissed off. She says when it's finished Doña Luisa will live better than all of us."

"Does Doña Luisa still talk about her privacy?" I asked.

"No," Julio said. "Not lately. And now my uncle wants to move into the new place with her. He wants to let Josefina and the kids take over his house."

"I guess that's for the best. Is Luisa getting along with Josefina?"

"Sometimes yes. Sometimes no," he laughed. "You know how that goes."

"Julio, if you're up for it there might be a way to earn a little extra money today." I pointed back toward the house. "We're gathering plant material for the lab project. Do you want to help out?"

"Why not?" He shrugged. "Let's go."

Heading back to where the others waited by the porch, I hoped Don Rodrigo was ready to give Julio the rest of the money so he could finish Doña Luisa's house. Now was not the time to ask, but I promised myself that part of any income I got from Brad and Debra would go to the new house.

Debra sidled over to me and whispered that Don Rodrigo didn't seem to be in the mood to talk to them. "First, he showed us a few of the dried plants he often uses with his patient," she said. "But then he got distracted."

"He's coming off of a bad spell," I said. "His energy is not what it was, but we're here now. Let's try to make the best of it. The plants are here, and Julio and I will see what we can do."

It was time to work. As I read out the first names of the common species on my list, I asked the old man to point us to the best places to find the plant specimens. Julio, Doña Luisa and I would do the leg work. Brad and Debra stood nearby, their SUV hatch open, ready to label the leaves, vines, and roots. Looking down the steamy forest trail, my thoughts returned to those first days in Belize. On those early morning treks, I struggled to keep up with my mentor as he forged ahead, moving through the brush. Now he could only sit on the porch, holding the stout stick he needed to lean on.

Baskets in hand, Julio and Doña Luisa and I awaited instructions. "There, there," he cried pointing the cane. "Julio, you see where the copal vine hangs from the tree? Climb up and get that one."

Julio didn't look happy, but he deftly slithered up the tree and tugged on the vines. Too late, he realized he'd misjudged the strength of the branches supporting him. With a cry, he fell to the ground and lay there stunned until Ronnie sprang up, running to help his friend.

Rubbing his head, and shoulder, Julio begged off the project. "*Lo siento*, I'm sorry. Carrie, you'll have to do this on your own," he said. Without another word, he got his car and drove away.

Don Rodrigo, too, grew tired. Slumping back on his chair, he turned to me. "*Mi hija*, I don't think you need me. You can do this on your own."

With Julio gone, Ronnie stayed on the porch where he and Don Rodrigo laughed and drank. He'd lost interest in our project and I couldn't blame him. Still, it did my heart good to see him enjoying himself.

Brad and Debra exchanged looks. Things were not going well. Now it was up to me to guide the project. I grabbed a basket, and as many cloth bags as I could and walked to the edge of the forest. The job ahead weighed me down.

At the sound of a twig snapping from behind, I turned, overjoyed to see Doña Luisa following close by. "Carrie, *mi amiga*, come this way. I will help you."

She was no novice to gathering herbs and neither was I. Together we walked into the dense green forest. We would have a long, hot day ahead of us, but together we would get the job done.

Twenty Seven

Sitting in the lab, Debra, and Brad talked around their budget and the price they could afford to pay for my plant database all without giving any hints. Like most Americans, I grew up paying "price as marked" on whatever goods I bought. So, my first weeks in Belize, wandering the stalls of the open-air markets had been an eye-opener, especially when I realized I was expected to dicker for a price. It turned out to be a lesson in negotiation. I'd learned how to haggle then, and I was ready to do it now.

Grabbing at a number, I asked for fifteen thousand dollars right off. Brad didn't flinch before he came back with an offer of five.

"That's something of an insult," I said. "I'm giving you over one hundred plant species with a catalog of uses for every one of them. When I think about all the hours I spent on each plant, it hurts to do the math."

I still was in the dark as to their total budget, but one thing was certain, they were earning a substantial fee. Thinking about the work that went into my plant database, I calculated that my hourly rate would have been about ten cents an hour for the many months of work. And me with a Ph.D. to boot.

After much back and forth, we all agreed on a price of eight thousand dollars in US currency. I was ready to give them the data, but it was not an exclusive agreement. I would still retain rights for usage in the future and I asked them to sign something to that effect.

It wasn't a huge amount of money, but it would have been enough to buy a few acres of land nearby. Somehow, my hope of owning land, planting it and perhaps, setting up a clinic had faded. I was not meant to be the legendary American healer of my dreams, living and working in the jungle. But that didn't mean that there wasn't something else that I could do.

Of course, money hadn't been even a small part of my motivation. My parents never nagged me about using the money I'd inherited from my grandmother. It was the fall back money I'd been living on since I arrived, and now it was almost gone.

Negotiations over, I wrote up receipts for Brad and Debra to sign. As subcontractors, they, not the NIH, were acquiring the research. They were giving me $4000 dollars each from their personal accounts. Since plants can't be patented, no one could really own the data. I could still retain my rights to use it. I might not want to use it in the same way they were, but I was sure to find other purposes for my work.

Was I giving my work away? Probably, but I didn't feel like they were trying to screw me, really. It was just another case of laboring in obscurity, in this case by my own choice, a common situation for many other scientists.

Brad made a motion with his hands, as if pushing all the money business out of the way. "Now that's done, let's move on."

"I couldn't agree more." It felt like a weight off my chest.

"We're ready to start processing the plant material we collected. By my count we bagged leaves, stems, and bark from over fifty species. Carrie, did I mention that we need to create three duplicate sets of each plant sample to send to the labs for testing?"

"Once they're processed, where will the plant samples will end up?' I asked.

"For now, we're thinking NIH, University of Chicago, maybe Harvard. Your database is just the beginning, but it's getting us off to a good start," Debra said.

I was surprised she spoke up after her silence. I'd always sensed a sympathetic spirit in Debra, but as we'd negotiated, she stayed mum. Wasn't it her job, and her money, too? Should I have been surprised? Women in science have been notoriously underpaid and under-represented since the beginning. Only now were things starting to change.

"Carrie, you've done so much work here. I'm wondering why you never thought about submitting a scientific paper to one of the journals," Debra said.

I had to admit she was right, and I had no answer. "Early on, I did begin a couple of articles, but I got distracted and never finished them. I think I still have the first handwritten paragraphs in one of my notebooks."

Where had my head been? In the clouds, obviously. I always thought there would be more time. I hadn't attended any conferences, and after a few attempts, hadn't really stayed in contact with any professional colleagues. I had made some connections early on, but I was soon distracted, spending my time out in the field, absorbing all the knowledge and everything I could learn from my mentor. How had I been so detached, so oblivious to the outside world?

Brad and Debra thanked me profusely. Not only did they

already have over fifty plant specimens collected from the forest, but they also had significant information on others. They were closer to their goal and I hoped we were done collecting specimens in the wild.

"Now we're on a roll," Brad said. "Carrie, I don't know about you but I'm ready to celebrate."

"Do you want to join us for dinner?" Debra asked. "We found a little place in San Ignacio that has amazing Belize barbecue."

"Thanks, but I'm feeling a little bushed." A headache was circling my temples. I went off to find solace but for what I wasn't sure.

I'd forgotten to ask if the NIH, a visible part of the U.S. health establishment, planned to compensate the Belize government for their help. And what about the people of Belize? Was there any way they were being reimbursed by outsiders making use of their traditional culture and folk wisdom? It occurred to me that I should ask myself the same question.

As I sat in my room thinking of what I'd sold, a sense of futility filled my heart. *Does it belong to you? Are you any different than Roz?* Maybe, maybe not. I wasn't coming in and using the knowledge of the local people to turn around and make a profit, or was I?

True, I'd done hundreds of hours of work, but that was work I couldn't have done without Don Rodrigo. The discoveries, the healing practices, were not my own.

Didn't they truly belong to Don Rodrigo and others like him? Shouldn't I share what I had with him? The more I thought, the more I knew the answer was yes. This money was not just mine. It belonged to the people of Belize.

I found Gloria in her usual place at the check-in desk in the lobby of the Seven Sisters Lodge. "Carrie, everything OK? You're looking a little down in the dumps," she said.

"It shows?"

Not exactly what you hope to hear. Maybe the soul-searching was visible on my features. "I was feeling a little low," I said "But I think I came up with a solution for something that's been bothering me. Any chance you could cash a check for me."

"I don't usually do personal checks. But if it's not too big a check, I can make an exception. I trust you."

"OK, thanks. How about six hundred?"

"It'll have to be Belize dollars."

"Deal!"

Next day, I called Julio, asking him to pick me up at the lodge. On our way to see Don Rodrigo, he updated me on the building project. "Some progress, but not much. I need supplies," Julio said.

"Maybe there's a way to fix that." Smiling, I felt the money in my bag, and it was hard not to give away my secret.

As Julio pulled his car into the yard, we were greeted by the sight of Josefina leaning against a porch rail keeping watch on the grandchildren. Don Rodrigo waved and smiled from his chair, his cane resting nearby.

The new construction looked unchanged from a few days ago. "Can I peek inside?" I asked, pointing. "I didn't have a chance to see last time."

Purple clouds faded as the sun warmed the horizon. As we walked past the vegetable garden, a gang of parrots squawked at our intrusion. Julio proudly led me to the open doorway. Beyond the threshold there were sheets of plywood over the floor beams. When they wobbled underfoot, I decided not to go further but from what I could see, the construction looked sturdy and solid. "Beautiful," I said inhaling the scent of freshly hewn timber. "You made something from nothing, and you did it all on your own. When it's done, we should have a fiesta, a housewarming."

"When it's done? You mean if it is done." Julio picked up a hammer and returned to work.

"Don't lose hope." I turned, heading back to the where Don Rodrigo sat on the porch. Sitting beside him, I reached over, found his hand and gave it a quick squeeze.

"*Mi hija*, you are back," he said. "Are you here to collect more plants for your friends? Or did you just come to bring me some cerveza?"

"No cerveza, but maybe something a little better."

Josefina made a face and walked into the house. Through the open window, I could hear the bang of the cooking pots as she expressed her displeasure at my presence.

"What do you have for me?"

"I brought you something that will help Julio finish the house for Doña Luisa. Where is she?"

"She went home to help a neighbor, but she will be back in a few days and I want to surprise her, to let her see that I am keeping my word. I want her house to be ready."

With that, I reached into my bag and pulled out the envelope of cash. "Look inside. It might not be enough to finish the house, but I can bring more soon. It comes from the Washington scientists you met before. They paid me for some work I did for them. And don't forget, the rest of your money is still safe at the lodge."

Don Rodrigo peeked into the envelope, "*Mi corazón gracias.*" A tear rolled down his cheek. "Why do you give this to me?" he asked.

"Why? For all that you've given me. All the wisdom and all the time you spent teaching me, sharing your skills so generously."

Don Rodrigo called out to his nephew, "Julio, *ven rápido. Aquiesta el dinero.*"

Twenty Eight

Debra, Brad and I began our first day working quietly in the lab, making use of the equipment set up months before. It felt good knowing that these tools would be put to real use. There were dozens of bags of plant material to be sorted. I held up each one, naming it before placing it in a container. Don Rodrigo always kept his samples in cloth bags. But what could we do? We needed to work quickly, sorting through specimens, labelling them and transferring them to cardboard boxes. Brad was anxious to give the drying oven a test run before we used it on any of the specimens, we'd collected days before.

Outside, I picked an armful of leafy branches from the crepe myrtle bush that grew nearby. We set the oven on a low heat and we were ready to begin. First time around, the oven worked fine but just to be sure, we tried a second batch. It was all good! Soon we were ready to move on to the real work of the day, drying the plant specimens we'd gathered the day before under the gaze of Don Rodrigo.

The lab's long counters ran the length of the room, and we

used them to set up an assembly line. At one end, Brad would dry the plants in the oven, then Debra would mount the dried material on sheets of acid free rag bond paper. Once they were mounted, I would label and package each specimen for shipment. When the processing was complete, each plant sample would be sent to laboratories stateside for verification. They'd be cataloged using current scientific classification.

Shipment might be some weeks in the future, but, on our first day, we got off to a good start. Brad congratulated himself for having the foresight, before leaving the States, to have had the special paper and other supplies shipped direct to Belize. "Lucky for us," he said. "Fat chance we'd be able to find stuff we need here."

As we worked, Debra began to scratch her arms. Soon welts began to appear on her pale white skin, moving up her neck to her face. She was having an allergic reaction to at least one of the plants, but which one?

"Has anything like this happened before?" I asked.

"I suffered from pollen allergies when I was a kid, but I remember doctors saying I would grow out of it. I thought that was a thing of the past. Back then I got relief from antihistamines. I should have brought some with me, but it never crossed my mind," she said.

The irony wasn't lost on any of us. We would be spending our days knee deep in plant material. So far, we'd dried nine different plants. Without a filtration system, the drying oven must be releasing microscopic amounts of plant oils into the atmosphere. I racked my memory trying to think of a time when Don Rodrigo had treated a case of hives like hers, but I came up blank.

What about aloe vera? I ran outside and broke off stalks of the spiky succulent growing in a pot on Mel's veranda. "See if this will help," I said.

She rubbed the aloe gel from the broken stalk on her arm. "No! It's getting worse. I can't breathe," she wailed.

Brad started to scratch himself in sympathy. "This is crazy," he said. "Carrie, you wouldn't have any antihistamine here, would you?

Thinking of the one-room grocery store in the village, I shook my head.

"Ok, I remember seeing a sign for a *farmacia* near our hotel."

"C'mon, Brad. Let's go," Debra said. "Carrie, do you want come with us?"

"No, I'll stay here. Whatever it is, it doesn't seem to affect me. I'll keep going and record what we've done so far," I said. "Brad, just come get me on the way back."

Our first day in the lab was not off to the best start.

Hours later, I peeked outside. The compound was empty, and silent. Even the dogs were sleeping. Mel and Gabrielle had gone back to the coast in pursuit of their new hotel and restaurant venture. Ronnie looked around, "Since things are slow, I'm giving myself the afternoon off." He turned to the new guard, "Carlos, you're in charge. if you need me, I'll be at the café." I watched him drive out in Mel's jeep, leaving the new hire in charge.

My phone said five thirty. It would be getting dark very soon. *I should have gone with him.*

I looked around. Where was Carlos? The new guard seemed to have vanished. Taking a siesta, maybe? No way did I plan to stay in the empty compound overnight. I tried calling Brad's phone but got a message. Feeling desperate, I called Julio. No answer there, either. After half an hour, with no calls back, I decided to walk.

The Seven Sisters Lodge was a couple of miles east. It would be a hike. I'd walked from there to the compound before, but I had only done it in the morning. Usually, there was no traffic on the lonely dirt road, but, as I walked, a battered car appeared out of nowhere. It slowed down next to me. A dark-haired man hung his head out the window. "Taxi, *Señorita?*" The car was the worse for wear, but the driver looked harmless enough, I thought. Evening shadows loomed ahead.

"OK, I'm going to the village to meet my boyfriend," I lied. The village, a little over a mile ahead was halfway between Mel's compound and the lodge. "How much?"

"All rides are five dollars Belize."

I really hadn't planned on going to the village, but I didn't want to let this guy know there was no one waiting for me anywhere. With luck, I'd find Ronnie at the village café and get him to drive me to the lodge. Shadows grew as the sun dropped below the horizon. Opening the rear door, I took comfort in the fact that it wouldn't be a long ride.

The driver turned the car around, heading back in the direction I wanted to go. Cranking up the radio, he sang along to a sorrowful ballad of love gone wrong. As the song ended, a sad sigh escaped his lips. In the rearview, I saw him he wipe tears from bloodshot eyes.

"*Mi novia*, my girlfriend, I miss her," he said.

"*Lo siento*" I said. "I am sorry."

Suddenly, a red deer sprang from within the tree line. With a bellow, the driver hit the brakes. "*Bastardo,*" he swore. Too late, the car skidded toward the opposite side of the road, coming to rest at the edge of a ditch. The deer sprinted off into the bush on the other side of the road.

After angrily pounding on the steering wheel, the driver got out to inspect the damage. "*Pedazo de carro de mierda.* Piece of shit car." He kicked the fender over and over and the cursing continued. "*Maldito ciervo*, fucking deer."

Pasting a pretend smile on my face, I walked around to where he stood. The right front wheel hung over the edge of the ditch and the right rear tire was flat. Something told me my ride was over. I pulled five Belize dollars from my bag and held it out.

He grabbed the money from my hand. Even in the gathering dark, but I could see the anger in his eyes and now I smelled the alcohol on his breath.

"Just like all the women. You are all alike."

"What do you mean?" I asked.

"Wait until there is trouble and then you leave."

The hair on the back of my neck prickled. I sized up my opponent. *He's not that much bigger than me.* But he looked wiry. My intuition said run. Before I could bolt, he clutched my left arm, twisting it as he pulled me toward him. At that moment, I remembered something my father taught me when I got bullied in grade school. Making a fist with my right hand, I crossed my thumb over the joint of my index finger, swung my arm around in a wide circle and hit him under the chin. "Huh," he uttered, with a look of surprise. Then I kicked him in the shins and ran into the thicket.

Light was dim under the canopy. I ducked behind a Ceiba tree, praying to its spirit for protection. As I crouched and listened, the only sound was my heartbeat and my breath rasping in my throat. Then a light flickered. *His cellphone?* Feeling around the roots of the giant tree, I picked up a fallen branch, wrapped both hands around it and waited. My newfound weapon was not heavy enough to deliver a knock-out blow to the head. But if I could catch him off guard, I would go for the knee or the groin. Maybe the piece of wood could cause enough pain to allow me a few seconds to escape. *Which way should I run?* For sure, no further into the forest, but I needed to get away from the driver and circle back to the road.

"*Chica, Chica,*" he called. "You don't need to run from me. It's not safe for you here in the jungle. I have my phone so you can see." He was coming closer. Then a harsh scream tore through the dark. *"Aiiiyeh, la serpiente me mordió.* Wicked snake."

A snake bit him?

Was this my chance to get away? Running around the tree, into a clearing, I saw the driver writhing on the ground. In the cellphone's glow, light reflected off the pupils of a poisonous striped coral snake. The viper's spear-shaped head was still attached to his ankle. Part of me felt sorry, but my instincts said, run. And I did.

I careened past him, back through the brush, toward the road, running like I had never run before. As I gasped for breath, my phone rang in my bag. It was Brad.

"Carrie, I'm at the lab. This place is deserted. Where are you?"

"Brad, thank God. I'm on the road going east toward the village. Come get me. A crazy guy tried to kill me." I climbed up the embankment onto the dirt road. Then I changed directions, running back the way I had come, back toward the compound in hopes that Brad might find me sooner.

It felt like hours, but it could only have been minutes before the lights of his car bathed me in relief. Brad was alone behind the wheel. I waved my arms and he stopped. "Get in."

I threw myself into the car. "Just drive. Get me away from here." We passed the broken-down taxi. "See that car? The driver made a grab for me and I ran into the woods. Before he could find me, he got bit by a coral snake."

"Should we go help him?" Brad asked.

"That's up to you. Please, just take me back to the lodge first. I'm done."

Turned out, Brad was more of a boy scout than I thought. After he dropped me at the Seven Sisters Lodge, he went in search of the snake-bitten driver. Finding the car but no driver, he went to the village police station and reported the trouble. At the village café, he found Ronnie and told him what happened. Ronnie wasn't certain that there would be any follow up. And neither was Brad.

Twenty Nine

Was the karma in Mel's lab was working against us? Day One, with my new colleagues, we'd gotten off to a difficult start.The project itself was going fine until Debra left.Was it time for me to step back and let them work it out?

Day Two, Brad picked me up at the lodge alone. "Where's Debra?" I asked.

"She's in her room, poor thing, soaking in a tub of baking soda.We did find a drug store, *la farmacia* in San Ignacio.They had antihistamines and the pharmacist was nice, she also recommended the baking soda. Debra's trying both remedies. We'll see which one works best."

Debra needed another day off to recuperate. Who could blame her? That meant there were only two people to do the work of three, but Brad was ready and so was I.

As we drove along the route to the lab, it was a surprise to see two guys with thumbs out. Did they know they were trying to hitch a ride in the middle of nowhere? They waved us down.

Brad hung his head out the window. "Where are you guys headed?"

"We were looking for the caves near Rio Frio, but we must have got it wrong." A Texas accent told us they were Americans and so did their baseball caps, sneakers and tattoos.

"No, you're headed in the right direction," I said. "You just didn't go far enough."

"We have work to do," Brad said. "But I can save you a long walk. Climb in."

They piled into the back seat. "I'm Dave. This is Ed. We're from Austin, Texas. Believe it or not, we're trekking our way through Belize on our way to Costa Rica. How about you guys?"

"I'm from D.C., here temporarily to work on a project. This is Carrie. She lives here."

"Wow. You live here? That's so cool. What's it like?"

"Very different from Austin, I'm sure. Living here be can be hard, but there are rewards."

"It's funny we should bump into you two. We heard about another guy from the States who lives somewhere around here. Some kind of expat millionaire?"

On our way, we approached Mel's compound. In the bright morning sun, it almost looked like a resort, the high white fence surrounding the property. Beyond the guardhouse, you could make out the red tile roof of the main home surrounded by lush foliage.

"Wow!" Their eyes popped. "Who lives there?

"That might be who you heard about. His name's Mel Powers," I said.

After another couple of miles, I told Brad to pull over. "See that?" I pointed to a footpath through the brush. "Follow it until you come to a narrow footbridge over the river. Cross over and stay on the trail. After about a two-mile hike, you'll see a steep cliff. Between two boulders you'll see the opening to the caves. Sometimes there are guides there to take you in."

"Thanks for the directions." They climbed out. "Appreciate the help."

Brad made a U-turn and we headed back. As the gate came up, we pulled into the compound. "All by your lonesome?" I asked Ronnie as he emerged from the guardhouse.

"No, Carlos is around here somewhere. But no word from Mel. He was supposed to be back last night. I guess he decided to grab an extra day on the beach. Can't blame him."

"Did you hear about the new hotel he's looking to buy on the coast?"

"Yeah, Gabrielle told me," Ronnie said.

"Whatever. Maybe, we should take advantage of the quiet," I said. "If you need us, we'll be in the lab most of the day."

"Hear anything more about the guy with a snake bite?" Brad asked.

"Soon after you left, he staggered into the café. He could barely walk," Ronnie said. "I think somebody took him somewhere to get it treated, but I don't know what happened after that."

Mixed emotions washed over me. *Karma?* Part of me hoped the guy would survive but part of me felt justice had been served.

Brad and I picked up where I'd left off the day before. We were ready to complete yesterday's work on the plant material. After that we'd decide what the next steps would be. Brad said he hoped that Debra would be able to work by tomorrow. I had my doubts, but I kept them to myself.

A couple of hours later, the quiet was broken by the sound of a helicopter whirring overhead. I wandered outside. Looking across the road to where a chopper had landed a while back, I wondered. *Is that Mel and Gabrielle flying in?*

There was no real landing strip nearby. Mel would know that. Still, the chopper stayed up, continuing to circle for several more minutes. The dogs got riled up and there was little peace until I heard Ronnie say, "I can't take it anymore. Carlos, lock up these freakin' dogs." Finally, the aircraft moved away, and it was quiet.

Around noon, Mel and Gabrielle pulled up in a new SUV. Mel went into the guard station to talk to Ronnie and Gabrielle came directly into the lab. "Carrie, have you noticed anyone strange around here?"

I wondered if she meant the taxi driver. "Yesterday, there was a weird guy who harassed me, claimed to be a taxi driver."

"Crazy guy driving a gray wreck of a car?"

"Yes, how did you know? Scared me to death, I thought he was about to rape me."

"Driving in, we saw his car in the ditch back there. What happened?"

"I needed a ride when he came along. I didn't realize he was drunk until he tried to grab me. I ran."

"Carrie, I'm so sorry. I should have warned you about him before. His name is Enrique Diaz. He claims to be a taxi driver, but he's the local pervert."

"I won't forget him, for sure. He might not forget me either. When I ran away from him, he chased me into the bush and got bit by a snake."

"Poor you. But I'm not talking about him. The cops know all about him. Anyone else?"

"Why?" I asked.

Brad walked over. "A couple hours ago, there was a helicopter that drove the dogs crazy, but it was quiet otherwise. Probably sight-seers."

"Mel's nervous," Gabrielle said. "When we were on our way back from the coast, he thought somebody was following us."

Brad and I exchanged looks. An old Bible verse crossed my mind. *The guilty run when no man pursues.*

"No, except for the helicopter noise, it was actually pretty quiet."

Brad turned to me. "Carrie, I have to go back to San Ignacio. I got a message from Debra. She said there's a delivery for me from D.C. Why don't you keep going? I'll be back before quitting time."

"Ok, I'll finish up labeling the batch of plant samples from yesterday. That should keep me busy until you get back." We watched his car drive out.

Gabrielle nudged me in the ribs. "Nice guy. He's kinda cute. Do you like him?" she asked.

"We're just working together." I had to laugh. "Besides, I think he has a wife back in the States." When Gabrielle asked me questions like that, it reminded me that she was still just a kid, barely out of her teens.

"Oh, well. I thought he might be your type. I'd like to see you find a guy but it's tough, I know," she said pulling out her phone. "Want to see something really cool? It's the restaurant that Mel and I are planning to open."

More promises from Mel? More dreams that fall by the wayside?

I looked over her shoulder while she scrolled through her pics. When she'd found a good one, she pointed and held it out. "Here, look."

"Wow!" I had to agree that the palm-thatched bar extending out over crystal blue water looked spectacular. "It's gorgeous. You say Mel just bought the property?"

"Not yet. We're going back in a couple of days to make it final. And guess what? He wants to call the restaurant Gabby's. After me." She gave me an excited hug.

"Congratulations. I know this is what you wanted."

"I know. Having my own restaurant is a dream come true. Of course, my biggest dream is still to go to America. But since Mel told me he can't go back to the States until his legal troubles get settled, this is the next best thing."

"We'll have to celebrate."

Outside, Mel was calling Gabrielle's name. As she trotted off to do his bidding, I couldn't help thinking that she wasn't a bad kid, just gullible. Had she sold her soul to the devil? As I stood there looking after her, I realized that maybe I had too. At that thought, I hung my head and went back into the lab to finish up the day's labeling and packing.

The day's shadows grew longer. The air was warm and sticky. Clouds hung low over the distant hills. Even birds in the trees fell silent. Brad had not yet returned with the supplies and I'd done everything that was left to do. It began to feel like siesta time. My eyes grew heavy. When I couldn't keep them open any longer, I looked for something soft to use as a cushion. Finding a scarf in my bag, I folded it into a small square. Not much of a pillow, but it provided a little padding as I rested my head on the counter for a quick nap.

Just as I was drifting off, a loud crack shook me awake.

Was that a gunshot? Oh God, please don't let it be Ronnie having another episode.

That didn't seem likely. He'd been so calm, so stable since Don Rodrigo had helped the ex- soldier find a way out of the stress and anger.

What was it? I jumped up. Peering over the window ledge, I looked into the courtyard.

There was Ronnie standing tall, his weapon at the ready. "Stop right there!" Ronnie said, his voice loud and commanding.

Even craning my neck, I couldn't see who or what he was pointing at. Moving over to the right, I looked through the other window, toward the river. My breathing stopped at the sight of two men, dressed in camouflage gear. Holding automatic weapons, they picked their way through the brush.

Is this the Belize gang unit, here to bust Mel for something? My heart caught in my throat. I squinted at the two other men. Could it be the hitchhikers, the guys Brad and I picked up this morning?

It is them!

Now, instead of t-shirts and sneakers, they were wearing long pants, boots, bulletproof vests, and holding automatic weapons.

A tall, bearded man stepped toward Ronnie. Exuding macho, he held up a large photo of Mel. "This man, Mel Powers, is a fugitive and I have a warrant to search the premises, apprehend him and bring him to court." From behind, the two others kept their weapons trained in Ronnie's direction.

"What are you talking about, brother?" Ronnie said. "What court is that?"

"United States Federal Court Southern District of Florida. Mel Powers posted a bond of a million dollars eighteen months ago. He's wanted for fraud and charges of criminal negligence leading to the death of an American citizen. He failed to appear for his court date and forfeited his bond. We have reason to believe the suspect is on these premises. If you point out where I can find him, we'll take him peacefully and be on our way."

Across the yard, the dogs were going wild. That was nothing new but, penned up for once, they were unable to guard against intruders.

Carlos, the new guard, ducked past, heading around the back of the lab. Mel and Gabrielle were nowhere in sight.

"I doubt you have any jurisdiction here," Ronnie said. "That means you and your men are here illegally. I called the authorities and they're on their way. I'd advise you to leave."

Ronnie are you serious? Authorities? Surely not the local police.

"According to the documents I'm holding, Mel Powers failed to appear in U. S. Federal Court on charges of criminal negligence. That alone makes him liable for a prison term. In addition, he owes the company who posted his bail a considerable amount of money for failing to appear."

I noticed Carlos, his hands raised, facing an armed man who pointed a gun at this chest. As one of the men spoke, Carlos nodded, pointing toward the main house. Gabrielle's dark curls popped up at the window then, disappeared.

The two men moved toward the house: guns drawn. One stepped up onto the veranda, the other took off running around the rear of the house, toward the river. Ronnie stayed put near the guard station, in a standoff with the leader who still held the documents in one hand, a gun in the other.

I heard Gabrielle scream. Near the riverbank, someone shouted, "Halt, halt." There were gunshots and I prayed no one got hurt.

All was quiet as I crept out of the lab and hid behind a tree. Moving toward the gazebo, I came face to face with a sorry sight. There was the mighty Mel Powers, down on all fours, soaking wet, face and clothing streaked with mud.

"There's our fugitive," cried one of men, waving the gun at Mel. "He jumped into the river trying to make a run for it. But we were waiting for him there too. Hold him still, Jake, while I put the cuffs on him."

Gabrielle ran toward Mel. "Let him go. You can't just come in here like a bunch of criminals. I called the police. They'll be here soon. What are you doing?" Her face was streaked with tears, her thin arms flailing against the bulletproofed bulk of the bearded man who hold Mel down.

The leader took out his cell phone and made a call.

No one paid me any attention as I crept over to where Carlos lay crumpled on his side. "Carlos, are you shot?" I whispered. There was a gash on his head, blood on his face and his arm.

"No, I tripped on that tree root and hit my head on a rock."

He looked dazed. "I'll be OK."

Looking down, I still held my scarf in my hand. "Here, let's see if this will stop the bleeding," I said, winding it around his head.

Time seemed to stand still as the two men held Mel in their sights. The third kept his gun trained on Ronnie. Overhead the helicopter reappeared. It circled for a short time, the blades swirling up clouds of dust and leaves. The craft touched down in the middle of the dirt road and the two men hustled Mel out of the compound. The leader kept his weapon trained on Ronnie as he backed out of the gate.

Once the men pushed Mel into the chopper, the leader followed, ducking inside. As the door closed and the helicopter lifted off, Ronnie ran into the road, firing overhead in frustration until it disappeared. With that, Mel was gone. To no one's surprise, the local police never came.

Thirty

Ronnie walked back into the compound, his head and shoulders quivering as though he was living through a bad dream. "I've seen a lot of shit, but what the hell was that?"

On the veranda, Gabrielle sat clinging to the cushion from Mel's chair. Her chest heaved with sobs. "*Mi amor, mi amigo.*" The focus of her life had disappeared in an unidentified aircraft.

Carlos, looking dazed was still slumped against the gazebo stairs. The scarf I'd used to bandage him looked to have slowed the bleeding. "Are they gone?' he asked.

"Yes, they took Mel and they're gone."

"What was that? A drug bust?"

"No, they had some kind of warrant," I said.

"Can they do that, just grab somebody?"

"They did it. Who knows where they're taking him?"

Carlos inched his way up to a standing position. He looked down at his arm, hanging at an odd angle. "Godammit, what should I do now?"

"Lean on me with your good arm and don't try to move the other one. It might be broken," I said.

"*Mala suerte*. Bad luck. Less than a month on the job, and now this."

"Don't worry. There's a good bonesetter not too far from here. Her name is Doñã Luisa. She's staying with Don Rodrigo, Julio's uncle. Let's give Ronnie a few minutes to collect himself. Then we'll drive you there."

Slowly Carlos and I made our way to where Ronnie stood, gun still in his hand. He looked stunned. "Did you really call the local cops?" I asked.

Ronnie shook his head. "The cops? Are you kidding? Who had time? I just said that, but I hoped maybe Gabrielle did. The guy had a gun on me from the jump."

Gabrielle still hadn't moved, and I walked over to her. "Did you really call the police?" I asked.

"No, Mel told me they were idiots," she gulped. "He said never to call them, so, I didn't."

"At this point, it's history," I said. "In the meantime, an American citizen's been kidnapped. We need to contact the U.S. Embassy." I searched out the number and made the call. After some minutes explaining the crazy situation, a staffer put me through to the Security Officer. She gave her name as Dylan Meyer.

"Of course, it's illegal for a bounty hunter to come to a foreign country to apprehend a U.S. citizen," Meyer said. "Are you sure they were who they claimed to be?"

"Who could say? They had something that looked like a warrant, but I only saw it from a distance."

"Warrant or no warrant, they have no jurisdiction here, no legal right to act in that capacity. Have you reported it to the local authorities?"

"Not yet. Here, let me put our security chief on. He was closer to what was happening." I walked the phone out to Ronnie. "U.S. Embassy," I mouthed, handing it over.

Ronnie's hand shook, but his telephone voice sounded strong. He provided his full name, current job title, and established his past military credentials. "The warrant looked real from where I stood but I didn't get that close," he said. He described the three men and a partial ID number from the aircraft along with details of what he could see of their documents. "It did look kind of official. I remember seeing a seal from the State of Florida at the top of the page. Maybe that's where they came from." Ronnie gave as much personal description of Mel as he could, then the call ended.

"What are the next steps?" I asked.

"They want us to go there and make a statement. She said to bring any documents we can find," he said. "If we hear anything from them about a ransom, we're to call right away. But I doubt those guys are about a ransom."

"Right. We should go to the house and try to find Mel's passport and anything else that could help track his whereabouts. But first things first. We need to take Carlos to get his arm taken care of."

"How are you feeling?' Ronnie asked his fellow guard.

"Could be worse," Carlos said. "Glad I'm not shot, but I got a mother of a headache."

Cradling his arm, Carlos climbed gingerly into the front seat of Mel's new car. I ran to get the keys from Gabrielle, but she wasn't about to give them up. "You're not gonna leave me here," she cried.

"Are you sure you can drive? I asked. I had my doubts.

"I'm OK. Where do you want to go?" she asked.

"It looks like Carlos arm is broken. Doña Luisa from the village is staying with Don Rodrigo now. She's a good bonesetter. I'll show you where to turn. It's not too far."

As Gabrielle drove Carlos and I out of the gate, somehow, everything felt different.

Thunder clouds rolled in overhead and a wind picked up. A flock of parrots sought shelter in the trees.

Heading up the hill to the farm, a familiar feeling welled up in my chest and I felt some of the tension drain away. Beyond the vegetable garden, Doña Luisa's cabin, now with windows and a door, looked almost finished. I could see that Julio had been making progress on the construction project and I was glad that my cash contributions helped to make it happen.

I ushered Carlos up onto the porch and Doña Luisa emerged with a smile. She gave me a quick hug. "This is Carlos. He fell."

Before I could say more, Doña Luisa swept Carlos hair back off his forehead. Looking into his eyes, she touched him softly. "You had a shock. I can see it in your face. Does your head hurt?" Under her gentle gaze, Carlos' features began to relax. She guided him to a chair *"Sentarse tranquilo*, sit quiet and I will get you some hibiscus tea."

She motioned me to follow her into the house. "Some men came with guns," I said. "There was a struggle and Carlos fell and hit his head." I looked around. "Where is Maestro?"

"He went with Julio to get some tools to finish my cabin."

"It looks like your new house is almost ready," I said.

Doña Luisa gave my hand a happy squeeze. "Oooh, I love it. It will be done soon, and I can't wait." She poured the tea into a chipped white cup and took it out to Carlos. "Drink this," she said.

Once he drained the cup, she was ready to begin her treatment. Whispering prayers in a mixture of Spanish and Maya, Doña Luisa called on God and the nine spirits to help her. She rubbed the injured arm with what she called her 'sacred oil,' carefully manipulating the bones of the forearm back in place. A cry escaped Carlos lips and a tear rolled past his nose. Once the arm was straightened, she said, "Now we make the sling." She looked about the room. "*Nada*, I need a piece of wood." She pointed me outside. "Look over where Julio builds mi casa."

Fat drops of rain began to fall as I ducked through the door of the newly built house. Inside, I spotted a flat, thin piece of plywood that could support Carlo's wounded arm. On my way to where Luisa waited, I stopped to pull the clean laundry from the line so that it wouldn't get rained on.

Inside, I placed the clean laundry on the kitchen table and gave Doña Luisa the piece of wood to use for a splint. Measuring it against the injured forearm, nodding agreement that it was a good size. She selected a pillowcase from the pile. Making a ripping motion, she directed me to tear the white cotton into strips. But first, I found myself looking around for Josefina just to be sure she didn't see me do it.

Winding the clean cotton fabric around Carlo's arm, Doña Luisa tied it in place so that his forearm lay flat against the board. He gritted his teeth at the pain, managing not to cry out as I'd seen others do. "From now on you must sleep only on your back and be careful not to bang your arm," Doña Luisa told him. "Give it two weeks to heal good and then we will set it again."

The rain stopped just as quickly as it had begun. As the sun broke through the clouds, I felt the moment come alive as Julio and my teacher appeared. As Julio brushed the rain from his thick, black hair, he caught me staring at him. He gave me a wink and a smile. I blushed.

"*Mi hija*, where have you been? We have missed you. And who is this muchacho?" Don Rodrigo looked from Carlos to Doña Luisa and back again.

"Men came looking for Mel. There was struggle and they took him away," I said.

"Carlos, *que pasa, amigo*? Are you OK?" Julio looked concerned.

"There was some violence," I said. "Carlos got hurt."

Don Rodrigo nodded sagely. "Those who live like a panther in the jungle, always prowling, will find themselves captured by their own deeds."

How did he know these things? He'd only been with Mel a few times.

"When I worked in the rubber camps as a young man, we saw many like him, like your Mel. I am sorry to see how it hurt Carlos, but I am not surprised. How is mi amigo, Ronnie?"

"He's OK. It scared him, scared us all. There were a lot of guns. We're not sure what we should do now."

"It will become clear."

Doña Luisa sensed that someone else was injured. She looked outside at Gabrielle. "How is the little one?" She'd been sitting in the car the whole time, crying and scrolling through the pictures on her phone, mourning the loss of her dreams.

"She's sad. Mel, the man she hoped would take her to America, is gone. The bounty hunters took him, and I doubt he will ever come back." It was as if Gabrielle had seen her whole world come crashing down. Unlike Carlos' broken arm, I knew that her pain that would take more than two weeks to heal.

As we spoke, Julio walked out to the car where Gabrielle still sat. Brushing her hair behind an ear, a smile replaced her tears. A stab of envy shot through my chest.

Heading back to the compound, we stopped in the village in search of the local police. Their car was gone and the door to the small one-room office was closed and locked. I asked at the grocery store nearby, but only got a shrug.

Brad was at the compound with Ronnie, the two of them scanning video from the security system. Much of it was out of focus, but in the clearest footage, we could see the back of Ronnie's head as he faced the group leader standing with gun drawn. Shots of Mel as he was pulled from the river were blurry. There was no audio, but body language made the threats clear. As they moved into camera range, I could see that Mel's hands were clasped behind his back.

When the leader gave the high sign, the two other men frog-marched Mel off his property and into the waiting aircraft that would fly him away.

This is footage Mel would never want the world to see.

Ronnie wondered what to do with the footage, where to send it. "Before you do anything, make a copy," I said. "And send one to me, too."

Searching Mel's office, Ronnie came up with his U. S. passport and expired drivers licenses from a couple different states. As I thumbed through some of the legal documents and correspondence from a lawyer in Florida, I put most of it aside, intending to read it later. I hoped it would shed some light on what happened.

"Ronnie, you, Gabrielle and Carlos work for Mel," Brad said. "Carrie and I were just here renting the space for our work. I'm not sure how helpful I can be."

"Brad, I get what you're saying but my situation is different. In the not-too-distant past, I worked with Mel too. He and I did have a contract."

I turned to Ronnie, Carlos, and Gabrielle. "My project with Mel didn't take off but I still feel committed to helping you guys out any way I can. The local police are useless but let's see what the embassy comes up with. In the meantime, I have a contact in Florida who might be able to steer us in the right direction." I was thinking of Laura, the Miami reporter who'd interviewed Mel. "I'll email her, give her the name of Mel's lawyer and see what she can find out."

Brad spoke up. "Carrie, if you plan to hang out here, I get it, but I might have to split. I can pack up what we've done so far."

"No reason we couldn't keep working here."

"I just called Galen. With the Christmas holidays coming, their lab will be empty. I'll be able to finish up there," he said. "Debra and I may have to rethink our next steps," he said. "We have more work to complete our initial NIH contract. We'll reevaluate, see what more we should do. I'll keep in touch."

He and I went back to the lab and boxed up all the samples we'd dried, packaged and labeled. The first samples were ready to send off to the States.

I helped carry the boxes out to the car. "Give Debra my best," I called as he drove out.

Thirty One

Ronnie followed up with the Chief of Security at the U. S. Embassy, making an appointment for all of us to give our statement. For most of the trip to Belmopan, Gabrielle dozed in the back seat and I sat up front holding Mel's passport and the other documents we'd found. There was also the security camera footage from that day copied onto a flash drive. I was hoping that someone at the embassy might be able to get the blurry images into focus.

After Hurricane Hattie all but destroyed Belize City years ago, the capital moved inland, and the city of Belmopan was created. The American embassy, located in the center of town, struck me as one of the larger and more substantial looking structures. The newish four-story building occupied the center of a large square block, not far from the Belize National Assembly and the Capital Building. Across from the American embassy, a gated compound, flying the stars and stripes was complete with tennis courts, and a sparkling swimming pool. Not bad, I thought. *The U. S. embassy employees look to have a pretty sweet deal here in Belize.*

Walking up the steps, Gabrielle grabbed my arm in what I took to be a case of nerves. As we entered the well protected structure, Ronnie seemed right at home, saluting the Marines on guard duty and answering their questions about our reasons for the visit. As directed, we passed through the lobby's metal detectors, heading up the grand stairway to meet security chief, Dylan Meyers, in her second-floor office.

We turned over Mel's passport and all other documents, including correspondence from his law firm that listed the partners names. Meyers spread everything out on her desk, taking time to read the contents. She held up one of the lawyer's letters. "Ok, can't blame the lawyers," she said. "This letter from three months ago confirms the date and time of the trial. He had plenty of time to prepare and make arrangements to be there," she said. "Apparently they wanted to meet and take his deposition before the trial," she said, lifting an eyebrow. "Did that happen?"

"I'm not sure. It's possible that the lawyers might have flown down before-hand." I turned to Gabrielle. "Did Mel mention meeting with his lawyers to you?"

Gabrielle looked a little frightened. "Mel talked about meeting a lawyer when we went to the coast to see about buying the restaurant. I just thought it was just about that property." Her voice shook, "I don't know anything else."

"But didn't he tell you that he couldn't go to the U.S. because of legal troubles?" I said.

Tears welled in her eyes, but Gabrielle shrugged and said no more.

After more questions, Ronnie pulled out the flash drive he'd brought along. Ms. Meyers plugged it into her computer, and we watched fuzzy footage of Mel, wet and streaked with mud, being pulled out of the river, handcuffed and led away by the bounty hunters.

Feeling we'd done all we could, we promised to check back if there were any other developments. Making our way outside into the sunshine, Ronnie, Gabrielle and I decided we'd earned a break.

Christmas was coming and it was market day in the middle of town. The day was bright and clear, the temperature balmy for a December day. A large evergreen tree, festooned with lights, stood tall in the middle of the town square. Brightly costumed musicians pranced from stall to stall, singing and dancing in celebration of the holiday soon approaching. The streets were awash in colorful stands displaying a rainbow of fruits and vegetables coaxed from the fertile tropical soil. At the very least, I promised myself a mango ice. Before I could find my favorite frosty confection, I was drawn to the fragrance of spicy chicken tamales. Exchanging glances, the three of us joined the line of hungry people waiting to sample the peppery treat. Tamales in hand, we found shade under a grove of banana trees. I noticed Ronnie and Gabrielle sitting close. As they ate, their hands brushed lightly, both of them smiling.

Even before I had a chance to reach out, the Miami Herald reporter got to me first. "What's the story on Mel Powers?" Laura's email asked. She'd attached a photo of Mel walking into the Federal courthouse in Southern Florida. "This is a big difference from the last time I saw him," she wrote. He was flanked by his lawyers, smiling, wearing a suit, and no handcuffs. A Miami Herald headline screamed, "American Businessman Kidnapped".

In his defense attorney's version, Mel was the former businessman who'd gone to an underdeveloped nation in hopes of doing good. Quotes from his lawyers described Mel's economic development work on behalf of the Belize government to the benefit its indigenous people. They claimed the jobs were close to being created, thanks to Mel's entrepreneurial skills. But I could have laughed out loud.

I thought back to early reports Mel sent to the Belize Department of Economic Development. The most he'd come up with was a video of green juice swirling in a flask, and the claim that it was an antibiotic formula based on plant material from local sources.

According to the Miami Herald, once he was returned to Florida, Federal marshals held Mel for two days. A back injury suffered during the kidnapping, had him hospitalized for a week or so before he was released.

"Do you know anything more about this?" the reporter asked me in a follow up call.

"Yes, I was there when it happened. There were three men with guns. There's video."

"Video? Can you send it to me?"

"If I can. They might want to use it as evidence. Mel's lawyer got in touch with our security chief, Ronnie. He wants to subpoena him as a witness. Do you know who hired the bounty hunters?" I asked.

Laura shot back, "It was the insurance company who paid his bond. They were based in the Cayman Islands. The courts might well frown on them sending bounty hunters to another country. That's illegal. So, lots of luck to them. For sure, the company will face charges for that. And I doubt they'll get any of the bail money back from the courts. Still, it makes me wonder if they were sending a message to their clients who might think about jumping bond. It's a crazy stunt but I give them credit."

"Give who credit?" I asked.

"The company who paid his bond. It might have been illegal, but it's a high-profile case and it was a way to get him back in the country. I'm working on a follow up article. When it's finished, I'll send it. Thanks for the inside scoop."

Later that day, Laura sent me what she'd written. The headline read, "Bounty Hunters Return Entrepreneur to Face Trial." Since Belize has no extradition treaty with the United States, they questioned whether that was a factor for Powers' decision to settle there. I had to laugh at the final paragraph. It mentioned that the bounty hunters had been charged with kidnapping but were now out on bond. *Tables turned?*

"Here's something for your scrapbook," she quipped, sending mugshots of the three bounty hunters as an attachment. "Thanks for the gallows humor," I shot back. For a minute I wondered if I should show them to Ronnie but decided against it. I was sure he could remember them all too well.

The Belize newspapers and TV news were full of the same story. As I watched it in the bar at the Seven Sisters Lodge, there was talk of little else. Soon I found myself surrounded by the lodge staff and guests, all buying me drinks, listening to the full story. I'd never felt so popular or so tipsy.

Two days later, Ronnie called to tell me that the Belize government had seized Mel's property.

"How can they do that?"

"Mel received a grant of a hundred thousand dollars from the government. In return, he promised to create dozens of jobs," Ronnie said.

"I knew he'd promised jobs, but who would ever imagine that he would promise that many."

"For sure. The agents who came to lock up the compound told me that before he got the money, Mel had to sign a performance clause. He was supposed to begin hiring some months ago. If that didn't happen or if he didn't repay the grant, he had to forfeit the collateral. In other words, the Belize government could take over the property. And as of yesterday, they did. They ordered all of us, Gabrielle, Carlos and me to leave. We only had a few minutes to grab whatever we could before they padlocked the place. One bit of good luck, they didn't get Mel's SUV, but I did." He laughed.

"Where are you right now?"

"We're at Don Rodrigo's farm. Carlos wanted me to bring him here so that Doña Luisa could look at his arm and fix the splint."

"How is Gabrielle?"

"About like you would imagine. She was in pretty bad shape. But since we got here, I've done my best to cheer her up some." He laughed.

"Keep up the good work, she's been through a lot. Do you have a plan for what comes next?" I asked.

"Not sure, I'm pretty broke. Mel hadn't paid us for a while. Trying to figure out a way to get home."

"I'll loan you the money for a ticket. You can pay me back whenever."

Thirty Two

"Brad, can you help me out? I'm trying to get an appointment with the Minister of Economic Development."

"Why would you want to meet with him?"

"It's complicated. I guess you heard Mel's property was confiscated by the Belize government?"

"No, I didn't. It was pure luck that I cleared out all of our materials when I did."

"You're right. I didn't even think of it."

"Can they just take a property like that?" Brad asked.

"Who's to say? Laws are different in every country. When Mel got a grant to create jobs, the Belize government asked him for a performance guarantee. They gave him a big chunk of money, so he must have offered his compound as collateral. But he never came through with the jobs. With him gone, they took it. There was no one to stop it."

"Sounds crazy," Brad said.

"Anyway, I was hoping that maybe you and I could meet with the minister. You could bring him up to date on how your project is going. And then I could try to find out what they have planned for the property."

"Knowing how things work here, I doubt the minister has Mel's property on his radar. I'd be surprised if anyone has given it much thought."

"It's been all over the TV news and in the press. It would be hard for anyone to miss it."

"But don't forget, beautiful as it is, that land is in the middle of nowhere."

"How is your project going for now?" I asked.

"Believe it or not, I'm at the Galen Science lab right now. Classes are over for the holidays. They're giving me all the hours I need until the new semester starts in the new year. But things could be better." He let out a sigh. "Debra was advised to go home. She left yesterday."

"Will she be back?"

"No, she's decided not to return to Belize. With the allergy thing, I can't blame her," Brad said.

"Sorry to hear that."

"I think she'll be OK, but her involvement in the hands-on research is over. She'll just handle the paperwork, stateside."

"So, where does that leave you?"

"I'm trying to finish up with help from the Galen Science Department. And I'm grateful for the connection. So once that's done, I'll send a final memo to the Belize agency before I go back to the States. I'd be willing to give you a ride to the capital. But I doubt I can help persuade anyone what to decide about Belize real estate."

"The property has value in a lot of ways. Don't forget about the lab and all the equipment."

"True, but it's not my business. Carrie, it's not yours either."

"If left to the elements, the jungle could creep in, overrun it in a matter of months. The rainy season is coming. I'd hate to see it be destroyed."

Julio and I rode out to the compound to take a look. On the gate, large signs issued a warning. "Trespassers will be prosecuted to the full extent of the law. Belize Department of Economic Development." I read it out. "Sounds serious."

The new locks on the security gates didn't budge, so Julio was all for climbing over the wall. "We don't have to do that, there's another way in. Just drive another mile or so down the road. There's a trail to the river," I said. "If we had wading boots, we could hike along the riverbank and get in that way. Let's go get some."

Julio pulled a face. "OK, but what if you slipped and fell in? The crocs would be waiting for you." Opening and closing his mouth and clicking his teeth, he mimicked the gaping jaws of the ever-present river inhabitants.

He was right. There were more than a few crocodiles lurking in the water, waiting for a meal. "What about a canoe instead?" I asked.

Next day, we were back with a canoe tied on the roof of his car. Parking near a stand of trees, we used the small boat to paddle downstream. All was quiet as we tied up behind the compound and climbed up the bank. At that moment, I wondered if some people might consider us to be the trespassers the signs warned against, but we found out that we weren't the first.

At the main house, locks were jimmied, doors kicked in and windows smashed. Inside, the computers, televisions, and kitchen appliances were gone.

"We weren't the only ones who knew the way in," Julio said.

I ran out, making a beeline for the lab. Aside from an overgrowth of grass, and brush around the edges, not much seemed changed. "Thank God, it's still locked." I said as Julio tried the door.

Slipping the key into the lock, we were inside. I ran my fingers over the countertops. Next, I opened doors to the oven and the refrigeration unit. "No lights in the refrigeration unit," I murmured to Julio.

Julio flicked the switch. "The power is off. I'll try the water,"

As water gushed from the faucet, a green lizard scampered up the wall, slithering into a crevice in the ceiling.

The water pipes Julio had run from the house were still in service. "I'm surprised they missed it," I said.

"Missed what? You mean the water pipes? I don't think so. They're copper, and somebody will come back for them one of these days."

"No, I was talking about the lab equipment. Whoever it was didn't know what it was worth. But what if they come back?"

"Trust me, they will be back," Julio said. "There's always a next time. We need to find a safe place somewhere for this equipment. Maybe store it at the lodge?"

"But it doesn't belong to us."

"Doesn't belong to them, either. Whoever they are, they'll be back," Julio said.

"Scavengers? Looters? Could it have been people from the village?"

"Who knows." Julio lifted the drier, testing its weight. "This stuff is too heavy for the canoe. I'll get a bigger boat and come back," Julio said. "I'll have to go all the way to Rio Bravo to get it. Do you want to come with me?"

"Better if I stay here. I can lock myself in the lab," I said. "I'll be OK."

"That's crazy. I might not be able to get back here before dawn."

"I have my phone." I held it up. "Anything happens, I'll call you or I can call Ronnie. He's close by and he has Mel's car."

As I watched him paddle back up stream, intuition told me it would be a long wait. The sun threw long shadows through the trees. Before darkness fell, I realized that I would spend a hard night on the floor of the lab.

I scouted out the main house for useful items. Grabbing a pillow and couple of quilts. I found the stub of a candle on a dresser in the room where Mel and Gabrielle slept. Snooping, I opened the nightstand drawer. It held a hash pipe, some matches and a scattering of pills. Wondering how the looters missed these, I promptly grabbed the candle and the matches, pitching the drugs in a trashcan.

Scrambling in the kitchen for anything edible, I came up with some crackers in a drawer and a can of soup. I ate the soup cold and gobbled the crackers, washing them down with water from the tap, thankful the water pipes were still intact.

Jungle sounds, and the cries of birds were my evening companions. Mosquitos buzzed outside and a spider continued to spin its web across the window screens. With the power off, I was grateful for the candle and the lock, secure on the lab door.

Early morning brought the welcome chug of a motorboat close by. Splashing water on sleepy eyes, I ran to the riverbank in time to see Julio tying up a flat-bottomed boat, the kind that took tourists downriver to view wildlife.

"Where did you get this?" I asked, thrilled by Julio's survival skills.

"It belongs to a friend. I helped him do some repairs on it, so he owes me a favor."

I thought back to the day the lab equipment was delivered, trucked in from the airport in a yellow DHL van. That day, months ago, Julio and I carried it into the lab, and it had felt like a new beginning. Now it was time to carry it out.

"You're amazing. How could I do this without you?" As I grabbed his arm in a thank you squeeze, he turned suddenly and clasped me to him. I felt his strength as our bodies connected for a heated moment. In a panic, I froze.

His eyes searched mine. "I've seen how you look at me. Why are you so afraid of your feelings?"

I pulled away, sadly considering the question. There were a few teen-age crushes, and a few college lovers. But my relationships, such as they were, seemed juvenile. Feeling light-headed, I stepped back. "We don't have long, maybe we should load up...."

"Why always work, work, work? I have never met a woman like you."

Not sure how to defend myself, I looked down. "When I was younger, in school, I was always the studious one, I was kind of a book worm. Not part of the 'in crowd'. It bothered me then, more than I would admit, even when I pretended not to."

He stopped my words with a gentle finger on my lips. "Don't be sad. It's not your fault." His hand moved over my shoulder, pulling me closer. "I am convinced it is because you have not known the right man."

I lifted my face to his, and all the nerves in my body sprang to life. In that moment, he was the right man. How had I not seen it? With no place to hide, my barriers fell. I felt the slow warm spread of something electric.

We kissed then, his face so warm and smooth that I wondered if he'd shaved. He ran his hand through my hair and took tiny nibbles of my earlobe. As his lips he found the sensitive curves of my throat, I was faint with pleasure.

As I leaned back against the counter. Julio's strength supported my body, his arms encircling my waist as we slid down onto the softness of the quilt still unfolded on the floor. The briefest thought floated by. *I never expected to use the lab this way.*

Like survivors of a shipwreck, Ronnie and Gabrielle were adrift. With Ronnie, sleeping in the back of Mel's SUV and Gabrielle bunking in the new cabin built for Doña Luisa. To Julio's relief, the construction work was done, and he was grateful for Ronnie's help in painting and installing the drainage system.

Josefina didn't like having extra people round, but Don Rodrigo did, and his enjoyment of these fun young people overrode his granddaughter's displeasure. Avoiding Josefina was a game I was used to playing. On my latest visit, I gestured for the Ronnie and Gabrielle to follow me over to a shady spot under the trees where we could talk in private.

When the three of us were together, we were like members of a group therapy session who'd been present for a trauma event. "What's next?" I asked Ronnie. We stood in a circle, fanning ourselves.

"Not sure. Right now, you know I'm broke," Ronnie said. "But I'm thinking maybe I could sell Mel's car."

"But you don't have any papers for it," I said.

"I doubt that would be a problem here in Belize. It's new, it's shiny and I'm betting that if I drove into the village, somebody would offer to buy it. Lately there's been a fair amount of cash floating around from drug sales."

"So, I've heard."

"They won't give me what it's worth but I'm not trying to make a big payday. I just want what I'm owed on my back wages and the cost of a plane ticket home to Florida."

"I can't blame you for looking for a way out of this situation, but don't you think at least half of what you get should go to our friend, Gabrielle?"

"Of course, we already talked about that, didn't we?" He gave Gabrielle a playful tug on a lock of her hair.

"Yes, we did. I might need money for a ticket, also," Gabrielle said, pushing him away playfully.

Ticket to where?

"But for now, I need some work and a place to stay," Gabrielle said. "Carrie, could you put in a good word for me at the lodge?"

"I'll ask Gloria, she's always looking for help. I'll be happy to vouch for your cooking," I said.

"What about me?" Ronnie pulled a frown. "Do they need anyone to do security or construction? I've got skills," he said. "Just ask Julio."

"I can see that. If you want, I can call James and Gloria. Maybe one of them would have time to see you today."

I dug out my phone and made the call, catching Gloria at a good time. "You're in luck. If you can get there before they start the dinner set-up, she can see you both."

Gabrielle looked down at what she was wearing. "Let me go change first. C'mon, Ronnie, you, too."

I heard a yawn and movement from the porch. "Ah, Carrie, *mi hija*. I didn't know you were here." The teacher rubbed sleep from his eyes.

"We didn't want to wake you," I said. "You looked so comfortable, but I wanted to ask you a question. What do you think about Mel's property?"

"It's very nice," he said.

"Yes, it is nice. Do you think it would be a good place for a school?"

"A school, *para los niños*?" he asked with a puzzled expression.

"Yes, I want to set up a school," I told him. "The idea came to me last night. It would be a place to teach the younger students about the traditions of your people and their ways of healing. What do you think?"

"No, no, no," he frowned, shaking his head. "*Demasiado trabajo.* Too much work. I cannot do it."

"You won't have to do anything. You've already done the

work, over the years. I treasure all that I learned from you. And now think of all that you've taught Julio. And there was, the meeting where they gave you the award and everyone clapped for you?"

"*Si, si, si,*" he said, the beginning of a smile breaking across his face. "*Si, ellos estan mis amigos.*"

"Yes, they're your friends and there are many others like them who might want to be part of the work, teaching others. Doña Luisa, Julio, and I will do whatever needs to be done." As those words spilled out, I realized, in my enthusiasm, that I hadn't yet asked them. But first things first. "If you give your permission, I'll write a letter to the man who gave you the award. You remember, the man with the big moustache, the minister? He's an important leader. He works in a building in the capital. If you'd like, you can sign the letter before I give it to him."

"No, no, no. My eyes hurt. I don't want to read it."

"Don't worry, I'll read it to you," I said. He was touchy about his reading. "We'll ask him to help us. You always talked about the schoolchildren. Remember how sad you felt because they didn't know the history of their people? You wanted them to learn about their heritage."

He cocked his head to one side, as if considering the idea, but stayed silent.

"Perhaps, we could even bring students from the college in San Ignacio and students from other countries. There is an interest in the work that you do."

"How do they know about it?"

"Many people have heard of you. Don't you remember the two scientists who came here from Washington? You helped them gather the plants they wanted to use for research? They knew about you, too."

Don Rodrigo frowned.

"Why don't you believe me? As a student, I read a story about

Belize in a magazine. Your picture was there, and that's how I learned about you," I said.

"*Si, si, si*. Now I remember." Finally, he began to smile.

From that hesitant beginning, I was ready to move forward. Even though it made me squirm, I got back in touch with Jeff. His sabbatical over, a new semester was approaching, and he would soon be ready to go into the classroom once again.

If he was surprised by my call, I couldn't hear it in his voice. "Carrie, I'm so sorry we didn't get to say good-bye. I didn't plan on leaving like that, but everything happened fast."

"So I heard."

"Something crazy came up. My son had just gotten his driver's license. When he took the car out for the first time, he claimed he was going to the library. Instead, he and his buddies took it for a joyride. My wife thinks they were taking selfies when the car went off the road and hit a tree. The car was totaled."

Fortunately, no one was seriously hurt but his sidekick in the front seat suffered a few broken ribs. And my son broke a bone in his foot when he tried to jam on the brakes. Everyone at home was freaking out and I had no choice but to go back. Even before that, Roz and I were coming to a parting of the ways. But I put it all in the note I slipped it under your door. Didn't you see it?"

"No," I said. I was glad we were talking on the phone so he couldn't see the expression on my face. I didn't for one minute believe he'd left a note. Later, I told myself I should have thanked Jeff for helping me cut the ties that bound me to him. Now we were colleagues nothing more.

"I read about Mel getting kidnapped by bounty hunters. That blew my mind. Is he coming back to Belize?"

"Mel won't be back. The property was confiscated by the government and things are pretty much up in the air."

"What about you?" he asked. "What are your plans?"

"Not sure. It depends."

"Why don't you think about writing some articles? I'd be happy to review whatever you have before you submit to journals."

"Maybe that would help."

"Help what?"

"I came up with a plan for opening an educational facility. I want to create interest that would draw people in the healing professions to Belize for a first-hand learning experience. Do you think it would work? There's got to be a foundation that might support it. And I think I might have found one."

"Wow! What a great idea. Of course, it will work. Let me spell it out for you," Jeff said. "Number One, traditional medicine has a kind of a fascination to it and there are many believers. Number Two, Belize is a pretty cool vacation spot. People are intrigued by everything about the place."

"Do you really think so?"

"I know so," he laughed. "It's like a neon sign that says, 'Come on down'. Look at you. Once you got to the jungle, you never really came back."

"I guess you're right."

"And, Carrie, don't you already have a perfect teaching tool?"

"What's that?" I asked.

"The list you told me about; the plants used by the Belize healers. You could use it to teach from. All you have to do is to put it into a workbook format and you're ready to go."

"Never thought of that, but you have a point. Maybe you could think about editing it for me?"

"We'll see. I can imagine many people would jump at the chance to study at a center with Don Rodrigo's name on it. I can't promise you any college students for the next year," Jeff said, "but I think the interest could be there. Let me know if you want me to write a letter of support to include in the grant application. It's the least I can do."

"Great. Maybe you can help. I'll send you an outline of what I have so far. And how about being on the board?"

"I'm in. See how far you get and keep me posted."

With Doña Luisa's cabin complete, Julio gave himself time off. "You deserve a break, meet me at the lodge and we'll kick back and spend the day together. And bring your bathing suit."

"I would but I don't have one."

"Go to the market, find one in the stalls. You're the resourceful one."

After a pleasant lunch outdoors, we wandered the grounds. Certainly, the sight of couples walking the fragrant, flowering paths arms entwined was nothing out of the ordinary. Seeing us, Maria smiled and waved as she went about her chores. Maybe I just never expected to be part of one of those couples.

For Julio, too, it was a new experience. "I never thought I would see myself as guest in a place like this."

We walked near the falls. "Now that you have more time, maybe you could come here and play guitar. When they have a lot of guests, James brings in musicians. If you want, I can ask him about it."

"Yes, I can use some work."

I pinched his arm. "I think I might have some work for you, too."

Overhead, clouds crossed the sun, throwing shadows. Julio looked up. "It looks like it might rain. Perhaps we should go to your room." He gave me a knowing smile.

"Are you afraid of a storm?"

"No, I just don't want you to get struck by lightning."

I do feel like I have been struck by lightning.

The fronds of a banana tree overhead dipped in the first breath of a storm. "Let's go." Running ahead, I grab his hand. "This way."

I opened the door to my cabin. "It's a little messy. I don't get housekeeping too often."

Like a kid, Julio peeked into the bathroom, picking up the towels and testing the fragrance of the shampoo and toiletries. He took a little bounce on the mattress to test it and then peered at himself in the mirror. As I joined him in the reflection, he put his arm around my waist, pulling me close. I leaned my head on his shoulder.

"You are beautiful, do you know that?"

And for the first time, I do.

I gave his chest a gentle shove as we fell back onto the bed together.

Sprawled and lazy, we lolled under the sheets, enjoying the breeze wafting in from the small balcony, the birds chirping happily after the rain. "Too bad we couldn't go for a swim. Next time," I say.

"Yes, next time. I hope there will be many next times."

"You made me forget what I wanted to tell you. I have some work for you."

"More driving?"

"Maybe, but it's more than just driving. Julio, I need your help. You heard me tell your uncle about a plan to set up a school in his name. I'm writing a grant, a kind of proposal, that might give us outside sources for money to do that."

"Money from where?"

"From an American foundation."

He looked a little downcast. "Well, I guess you won't need me to help you anymore."

"You couldn't be more wrong," I said. "If you're willing, we could make connections with some of the leaders and teachers in the villages. I have some names from the conference. Talking with them would be a good starting place. And you'd be terrific at that."

Whenever we could, Julio and I took to the backroads, taking turns behind the wheel of the old white sedan. Going from village to village, we connected with healers, midwives and schoolteachers. Julio's ability to converse in English, in Spanish and in the Mayan tongue was a blessing. Most of those we talked to were elated by an opportunity to see their legacy preserved and passed along to the younger generation. With their permission, we recorded their words in hopes of adding the comments to the still unwritten grant.

Driving gave us lots of time to talk. Reluctantly, Julio told me of his years growing up, sorry that he hadn't had much schooling. "I was never much of a student," he laughed. "I don't know much about a school. My mother worked as a maid and after my father died, she married my stepfather. He and I didn't get along. After that, I was on my own except for the few years I lived with Josefina."

"Tell me again how you are related to Josefina."

"My grandmother was Don Rodrigo's sister. Josefina married the son of Don Rodrigo's daughter who passed away. And I grew up with her son, Ramon and that's why she took me in."

"I'm glad she did. Was that after you left school?"

"I had a few years in the classroom. At least, I learned to read. My teacher told me I was pretty good at numbers, but that was before I had to leave school." He looked a little subdued.

"You have nothing to be ashamed of," I said. "There are many kinds of intelligence. You just happen to be a genius at putting things together. Look at the beautiful place you built for Luisa and how you figured out to give her the bath she wanted. To my way of thinking, you already have a college degree in "savvy." If this was another time and place, you'd be an engineer. Who knows, maybe you still could be, if that's what you wanted."

Little by little, I shared details of my more fortunate, but still stressful childhood. Our new openness made it easier for me to admit to being a nerd, to being teased for my lab experiments with plants and for my annual exhibits in the science fair. We shared a chuckle when I told him about my science experiment feeding hamburger to my Venus flytrap in eighth grade and how it grossed out some of my classmates.

But most of all we talked about what we might do if it we were to set up a school. While I thought we could make it happen, Julio was reluctant to place much hope in the outcome I prayed for. "*Es un tiro lago*, it's a long shot," he said.

I didn't like it when he said that. But I knew he was right. If things went as planned, we would need to go to the capital and beg the government minister for a guarantee to allow access to the property. We would need their buy-in before we went any further.

"There's one more thing. Even before we talked about this grant, I realized that I couldn't make it happen without you. So, will you work with me? Be the hands-on manager?"

"Hands on? What does that mean?" Julio leaned over, making a teasing grab for me.

"Keep your eyes on the road or we'll wind up in a ditch." I gave his arm a playful punch, followed by a quick peck on the cheek to soften the blow "C'mon, get serious. You grew up knowing the ways of your people. This is your culture. I came here to learn of its science and healing, but it's always been part of your nature and your spirit. Besides, you are *muy guapo.*"

"Yes, I agree." He mugged into the rearview mirror.

"C'mon get serious. The grant that I'm writing describes a plan in two parts. The first part calls for us to teach the younger children about your culture. The second part calls for teaching the high school and college students about traditional healing. We can both do that. My job will be to set up the lessons and the curriculum. Together we'll hire local people to help us find a way to connect with the culture and to help preserve it, so it won't be lost. You'd be great at that. Whatever they give us, we'll share fifty-fifty. What do you think?"

Maybe it was crazy, but now I was ready to begin writing a proposal letter requesting that, with the backing and knowledge of Don Rodrigo and other healers, the government of Belize would allow for the preservation of the confiscated property. It would be used to sustain the heritage and the indigenous culture of Belize. In return, I'd find a way to pay the government of Belize a minimal amount of rent and maintain the property.

The next day, with the letter written, I read it aloud to Don Rodrigo. Forehead creased, his mouth curving down, he listened without saying a word.

Doña Luisa sat close, holding his hand. "*La escuela*, the school must be named for you," she said.

"Oh, yes," I agreed. "I thought you knew. Did I forget that? It's an important part of the plan. Would you like that?"

A smile slowly began to tug at his lips. And with Doña Luisa's help, we teased a promise from the elderly healer. She even helped me convince him to go see the important man in the government capital. After Don Rodrigo made his mark on the letter, he insisted that Doña Luisa sign it also.

Once he gave his blessing it was time to celebrate. As soon as I could gather Gabrielle, Ronnie and Julio together, we stood outside together in the shade of the banana tree. I blew up balloons for the children and cut a cake from the Seven Sisters kitchen. Even Josefina was smiling.

"Julio, open the rum," Ronnie said.

"Let's toast the newest staff members at the Seven Sisters Lodge," I said. "The head chef has a job for Gabrielle. And Ronnie, James has work for you, too. He wants you both to start this weekend."

When all the pieces were in place, Ronnie found a couple hours to drive me to the capital, so I could hand-deliver my letter to the Department of Economic Development. I knew Julio was right. It was a long shot. Still, on the plus side, there was little benefit to the government in holding the property unprotected. With its remote location, the compound could quickly deteriorate or, worse, become a target for squatters, or drug dealers.

I included my email address in that letter, and happily received a reply before the month was out. When a date for the meeting was set, I asked Don Rodrigo, Doña Luisa and Julio to go with me to the meeting.

Doña Luisa and I talked about how to prepare for it and soon after I heard her try to convince Don Rodrigo to put on a long-sleeved shirt and tie. But he staunchly refused. "I will dress as I am," he said. "I am not ashamed."

Doña Luisa tried to make up for his lack of decorum by saying she would wear her best, a lovely dress of hand-woven fabric, embroidered in many colors.

Who am I to talk? I had serious wardrobe issues of my own. *What to wear? What to wear?* I asked myself as I peered at my skimpy choices. I'd hoped to make do with a denim dress bought some months earlier at an outdoor stall in the San Ignacio market. But when I tried it on in front of the mirror, it seemed to have shrunk. I couldn't call on Margo or Ellen for help. My more stylish friends were already back in the States in the classroom.

I missed my fashion advisors and their friendly laughter. And when I told Julio I had no one to ask for guidance, he surprised me by suggesting a shopping trip to San Ignacio. But this time, instead of shopping in the stalls, he wanted me to visit a store he knew, one with a dressing room. "This way, you can try it first," he said.

I thought back to my difficult teen years when Mom took me shopping. We were quite a pair. She would suggest something girly while I wanted to stick to the denim look favored by my peers. While my mother fumed nearby, I sat in the dressing room sulking, refusing to try anything on. My father often called us both a "retail nightmare."

Shopping was something I'd always tried to avoid but I hoped that this might be a different experience. "I need something for an important meeting," I told the shop owner. She asked my size and then scanned the racks, pulling out a few items. She ushered me into the dressing room and handed off the pieces she'd chosen to her assistant. Near the door, Julio sat quietly, smiling at me and nodding encouragement.

As I tried on selected outfits, the salesperson murmured, "Most men who come in with their girlfriends aren't so patient. Or so cute." Looking in the mirror, I smiled at my reflection. My final choice, a fashionable black cotton pantsuit, met with the approval of everyone in the shop.

On appointment day, I was ready to make a pitch to the new owner of Mel's compound, the Belize Department of Economic Development. Julio's car needed some work, so he and I packed a reluctant Don Rodrigo and Doña Luisa into Mel's SUV. With Ronnie driving us to our appointment in the capital, we were ready to go.

Unlike the U. S. embassy, the government building housing the Belize Department of Economic Development had no guards, no metal detectors, and no barriers in the first-floor lobby. Ronnie walked us up the steps to open the heavy doors for Don Rodrigo who leaned on a cane as Julio flanked him on one side and I took the other.

As Julio guided his uncle toward the lobby, Ronnie pulled me aside. "I have an errand to do at the U. S. Embassy," he said. "But that should only take a couple of minutes. I just need to pick up some paperwork. I'll be out front waiting when your meeting is over."

"Everything OK?" I was curious but it would have to wait.

"Never better," he said with a grin.

Inside the building, we saw a few casually dressed workers going about their duties, carrying files, chatting and drinking coffee from paper cups, like employees everywhere. The receptionist at the lobby desk smiled warmly at Don Rodrigo and Doña Luisa. As I announced our appointment with the minister, Enrico Santos, I wondered if we would be the most colorful visitors of the day.

The greeter slowly walked us to the elevator and pushed the button. When the doors opened, Don Rodrigo locked eyes with Julio. I knew he didn't like enclosed spaces, especially ones that moved. But Doña Luisa offered soothing words and we all stepped slowly into the lift. I pushed the 'up' button.

On the top floor, the minister greeted us, escorting my teacher and Doña Luisa to a small loveseat across from his desk. Next, he rounded up a couple of straight-backed chairs for Julio and me. When I took in his white, short-sleeved jersey with the Belize national seal on the pocket, his black pants and athletic shoes, I smiled, realizing that Don Rodrigo's fashion instincts were better than mine.

Perching on the edge of his desk, he looked in my direction.

"So, Ms. ..., I got your proposal." At a loss to remember my name, he looked for it at the bottom of my letter, sitting beside him on the desk. "Forgive me, how would you like to be addressed? Do you prefer Ms. Mullen, or shall I call you Dr. Mullen?"

"Dr. Mullen would be fine," I said, deciding today would be a good time to make the most of my title.

"OK, Dr. Mullen, then," said Mr. Santos, smiling broadly. "I have to say I was a little surprised by what you sent me. But now that I see all of you here in person, I do recall you and Don Rodrigo together at the Healers Conference."

"And *Señor*" he said bowing to Don Rodrigo, "I am most honored to meet with you again. Of course, I am familiar with your work. Who in Belize is not? In fact, my mother was a midwife in San Felipe. You may know her, Clara Santos?"

Don Rodrigo shook his head, but Doña Luisa's face brightened.

"*Si, si, si*. Minister, yes, I know Clara Santos. Many years ago, my friend, Rosa moved with her husband to San Felipe. Your mother, Clara, delivered her twins. The babies were large, and the birth was difficult. My friends always said that your mother saved her life."

As new connections warmed the room, the meeting took on a more friendly feel. Finally, there was a lull in the conversation and the minister stood and stretched, holding up the letter I'd written. "Dr. Mullen, you say in your letter that you are writing a grant that calls for funding for a school. Tell me more about that."

Dampness spread around my collar, but I prayed that my voice would hold firm. "With your permission, I have some illustrations that will make things clearer." I passed the visual aids I'd sketched to the minister. "Here's a diagram that shows the facilities on the compound. And here are photos of the main house, the gazebo and the laboratory. These would all be key parts of the project. In addition, there's an adjacent property that began as a small development of vacation homes. When the developer ran out of money, Mel, or Mr. Powers, bought it up. It has housing units that would be perfect for college students traveling to Belize for summer sessions. We're counting on that as part of our plan to create additional income."

As the pitch continued, I outlined job opportunities that could be created for the local economy. Cooks, grounds keepers, security, transportation, and cleaners would be hired to maintain the facility. In the educational realm, there would be employment for teachers, traditional healers, herbalists, midwives, artists and other cultural leaders who would teach the younger generation of their traditions and heritage.

"This is a lovely idea," the minister said, "but, please refresh my memory. Where will all this money come from?"

I ignored the condescending tone. "If the Belize Ministry of Economic Development will agree to lease us the land, I'm planning to apply for grant funding from the Central American Growth Fund."

"Ahh, yes," the minister smiled. "I am quite familiar with this well-known foundation in Washington, D. C. They have generously funded many successful projects in Central America."

I took the plunge. "Then with your permission, I'll forward the grant application to you for your approval very soon."

"I look forward to reading it."

Thirty Three

Days and weeks crept by, with my life on pause. The calendar pages I'd filled with important dates and scribbled deadlines, my constant companion as I waited for the response to my grant application. As we waited, Julio and I decided that action was called for.

Choosing to believe that the grant would become reality, Julio and I went out together, making contacts and forging in-person connections. He was our cultural ambassador as we traveled to the surrounding villages, introducing ourselves to teachers and community leaders. The first part of the project called for enrolling Belize public school students in workshops where they would learn more of their traditional culture.

Don Rodrigo's name on our project worked to open doors. At meetings with local schoolteachers, I asked if they included lessons on their culture, and the healing and the lore of the people of Belize in their lesson plans. Often the answer was no. When asked if this missing piece was something on their wish list for the students to experience, the answer, most often, was a welcome 'yes'.

On our weekly treks back to the compound, we watched as bits and pieces of anything portable continue to vanish. I was desolate but Julio was philosophical. "What could you expect," he said. "It's a poor country?"

Fearful that the plumbing would be the next thing to go, I called on Senõr Santos, at the Office of Economic Development. I begged him for more government protection of the property. Finally, he agreed to send someone to put new locks on the main house and board up the windows and doors.

I'd gotten in the habit of waiting for the daily arrival of the yellow DHL van that connected the Seven Sisters Lodge with mail and supplies from the outside world. Most days, around noon, I could be found in my usual spot on the porch, watching for the driver. He didn't know what I was waiting for, but he knew I was waiting for something important.

On a hot, sticky June day, the yellow van rolled in later than usual. Leaning out the window, the driver held up a large envelope. "Package for Dr. Carrie Mullen. That must be you."

I ran to the truck. The driver handed me the thick white envelope. "How about that?" he said giving me a thumbs up. "Didn't know you were a doctor."

I ripped open the package and tears stung my eyes as I read the official looking letter on top. After some months, the hoped-for response from the Central American Growth Fund had come through. The grant would fund the project for three years. During that time, there would be quarterly progress reports and a semi-annual online meeting with the non-profit headquarters in Washington D.C. to discuss future milestones.

I called Julio. "*Felicidades*. We got it. Now all we need is final approval from the Belize government. I hope we can make that happen soon. Are we partners?" I asked, touching the jade amulet at my throat.

"Partners, for sure. Let's go tell my uncle."

Soon there were other things to celebrate. Ronnie and Gabrielle both enjoyed working at the Seven Sisters. Their jobs provided money, meals and a safe place for each of them in the staff quarters.

Ronnie had no problem selling Mel's SUV. Gabrielle found a buyer, a host in the dining room who was looking for a car. Even if the SUV sold at a greatly reduced rate, the terms were cash on the barrel head. "I didn't ask where the money came from," Ronnie said. "The way things roll here. Sometimes, it's better not to know."

Before the car sold, on their days off, Gabrielle and Ronnie had driven to visit her family near the coast. Even though he didn't have money like Mel, Ronnie spoke good Spanish and he was polite and respectful. "My mother told me she thought he was better for me than Mel and he's more my age. She hurt my feelings when she said that, but maybe she was right. I like the way Ronnie treats me and he never yells," Gabrielle said.

Soon after, Ronnie took Gabrielle to Belmopan so she could apply for a Belize passport. Once she got it, Ronnie was ready to go to the next step. He could go to the American embassy and begin the process so that she could get the ninety-day visa.

"What's that?" I asked.

"Ronnie applies for a special visa for me. It's called the "fiancée visa". It lets me go with him to Florida. When I get there, I can meet his family and we can find a place to live. After that we have ninety days to get married. See my ring?" She held out her hand to show me the tiny sparkler on her finger. "It's a dream come true. Then I'll be able to get my green card and someday, maybe, I'll even become a U. S. citizen."

Thirty Four

One year later

The first school year for Don Rodrigo Montoya Cultural Center was ending. June would soon bring the rains. From the road, the compound looked much the same as it had been when Mel was the owner but inside it was different. The courtyard had become a parking lot for the school buses. The main house was converted to classrooms. My lab still housed some scientific equipment, but it was often used by students from Galen University who came with their biology instructors.

The gazebo Mel built in hopes of setting up a treatment program for veterans suffering from PTSD was now an outdoor space for performances by Mayan singers and dancers. Beyond the gazebo, a sturdy fence prevented curious students from exploring the riverbank and falling in. All these physical renovations had been planned and executed by Julio with help from local carpenters.

I was excited to see our numbers looking good on the final report for Year One. We had completed two hundred and twenty hours of education for elementary students and one hundred forty hours of classroom education for students at the secondary school level. I had several pages of positive feedback collected from the teachers to forward along with the numbers. We had met our first-year milestones as designated by the grant from the Central American Growth Fund. And Year Two would be even better.

We had kept our part of the bargain with the Belize Economic Development Office, hiring a dozen local people to work as cooks, cleaners, maintenance, guards, and teacher's aides. We had also provided paid work to members of the Belize Healers Association who came in to instruct the young people on how their healing knowledge has passed through many generations to play the role it continued to hold in their world.

Once the report went out, Julio would begin preparing for the first Maya festival we hoped to film and put on our website. He'd already contacted musicians and dancers. Many of the people who helped us make the Center happen were on the guest list for the celebration.

Over the summer we were expecting our first group of American college students to stay in our dorm housing. I reconnected with some of the academics like my former professor, Jeff. We made connections with teachers at Galen University and we hoped to partner with them for the upcoming year. We connected with midwives and nurse practitioners from the Midwives Council. With them we had hopes of attracting students in the healthcare field to Belize as part of an international studies program.

Summer vacation for the public schools would start next week. From my window, I watched Julio wave farewell to the last class of elementary school students as their bus pulled out. I wanted to jump up and down. Was Julio as excited as I was? Once they were gone, he burst into the office.

"Year One, we did it!" I cried.

"Yes, we did it," he agreed. He took my two hands in his strong brown ones and together we did a silly little dance, jumping up and down.

Moving closer, I planted kisses on both of his cheeks. He held me close. Looking into his dark eyes, I asked, "Friends, partners?"

"Yes, friends, partners," he said, holding me close. "And something more, yes?"

"Yes."

About the Author

Arriving in Philadelphia as a college student, Lee Fishman fell in love with city living and settled in. Even after traveling to Italy, Greece, France, Holland, Spain, Portugal, Morocco, Turkey, England, Guatemala, Columbia and Belize she still can't think of anywhere else she'd rather live than Philadelphia. Ok, maybe Paris.

As a student, fascinated by ancient civilizations, she spent time at digs and worked in an archeology lab piecing together pottery shards from ancient ruins at Tikal. Many trips to Central America, rekindled a fascination with the Maya culture and inspired her to write The Shaman's Gift

Other Books by the Author

Edge of a Dream. Escaping the war-torn city Sarajevo with only their lives, young immigrants, Rija and Josef arrive in America hoping for a better life. But when Josef, lured by dreams of easy money, takes off for Las Vegas, Rija must find her own way.

Mediums Guild. Margo takes her psychic gifts for granted, but when a young pilot asks for her help to find a missing loved one, Margo comes up short until a dream changes everything.

Follow on Twitter @leefishman1
On Instagram @leefishman.net

CPSIA information can be obtained
at www.ICGtesting.com
Printed in the USA
BVHW040004210421
605395BV00008B/1743